Seek the Risk

One Man's Journey into Non-monogamy

Recounted by Adam

© 2023 by Adam. All rights reserved.
ISBN 978-8-218-18652-4
www.seektherisk.net

Cover art by Arturo Mendoza Elfeo
@arteamelfeo

Contents

ACT I — 9

Chapter 1: Experience Hunting — 11

    Ladies and Gentlemen, the Bronx Is Burning — 24

Chapter 2: The Disruptions Are Where True Living Begins — 31

    Just When I Had Life All Figured Out — 34

    Course Set, Collision Inevitable — 56

Chapter 3: Wake-Up Call — 62

    Sand and Surf and All That Childhood Shit — 73

ACT II — 91

Chapter 4: Ignorance Is Bliss — 93

    I Do Until I Don't — 96

    The Worst Sound I Ever Heard — 106

Chapter 5: Adam In Wonderland — 111

Chapter 6: Cigarette Break — 129

    Signs of Stability vs. Signs of Instability — 135

Chapter 7: Time to Get to Work — 148

Chapter 8: Digging Deeper into the Toolbox — 157

Chapter 9: Fight Club — 169

    Let's Go to the Videotape — 179

    Am I a Fucking Adult Now? — 192

ACT III ... 197

Chapter 10: Hitting My Stride ... 199

    The Top Floor, Please ... 204

    Of Levees and Lightning ... 211

Chapter 11: Pride Kills ... 219

    Side Effects of Public Non-monogamy May Include… ... 236

Chapter 12: Growing into the Relationship That Jane Wanted ... 242

    Sometimes the Frog Notices ... 254

Chapter 13: All Journeys End ... 259

    Epilogue ... 272

Acknowledgments ... 275

This book is a memoir. The events have been recounted to the best of the author's ability. Names have been changed and some timelines have been compressed. All significant dialogue has been re-created with the help of the parties involved.

ACT I

Chapter 1
Experience Hunting

Excerpt from Adam's journal:

My feet settle gently on soft sand, and I am standing on the bottom of the Caribbean Sea, 104 feet below the surface, outfitted only with a dive mask. I slowly open my eyes to see a blue-green world of pure wonder. The rope that I used to guide me to this spot hangs in front of my face, snaking all the way to the surface buoy that it's tied to, and slowly moves back and forth from an unseen current. Several lazy fish are completely ignoring me.

The sunken cargo ship off to my right towers above me and I'm shocked at its size. It must be as tall as a five-story building, and I feel very small next to it. I look farther up to the surface, where the air is, and a wave of fear goes through me. *Wow, that's a long way up.* My heart rate responds to the fear and starts to increase. My brain's survival instinct is kicking in, demanding that I surround myself with air instead of water. I fight the urge to grab the line and make a panicked dash to the surface, which would burn the oxygen I have left at such a fast rate, it would likely cause the very thing my brain wants to avoid. Drowning. *Chill the fuck out, Adam!* I focus and start going through my process of reframing the experience. *I'm not scared, I'm exhilarated. Look at this amazing world you're in,* I tell myself. *You're totally fine and in control, you can hold your breath for over four minutes and you've been down barely a full minute. Enjoy it.*

The tension in my body eases, and I feel my emotions begin to relax. Continuing to force the calm, I take another look around, really acknowledging what is taking place here: that I'm standing in this stunningly beautiful spot on the ocean floor, deeper than I have ever dove (even with a scuba tank), feeling free in the way that I did the first time I jumped out of an airplane, but far more peaceful. With the weight of four atmospheres of pressure pushing down on me, my lungs are almost completely collapsed, giving me a distinct sense of the ocean's hug.

I slowly raise my hand and grab the rope in front of me and give a nice easy pull to start my rise to the surface, slowly scissoring my legs to use the massive fins I'm wearing to add a little extra thrust. Pull and glide, pull and glide, over and over again. "Stay in control," I repeat to myself as the diaphragm contractions begin in my body from the CO_2 building in my blood. Counting the contractions to keep myself distracted, I get to five, ten, fifteen, then they stop for a few moments before starting again with renewed vigor. Nice and easy, keep it calm, the surface is getting closer. I catch a glimpse of the dive watch on my wrist reading 55 feet, almost halfway home. Pull and glide, pull and glide. I see my safety diver swimming down to keep an eye on me during the final 30 feet, where a blackout is most likely going to occur if I've stayed down too long. Force the calm, force the calm. The last 10 feet glide by, my face breaks the surface, and I feel the sun while I take a big gulp of air.

I've made it back from a journey that seemed impossible when I first started, to a world I thought I could never go to. I've faced my fears and opened up possibilities for myself extending far beyond those precious seconds at the bottom of the sea.

I think every guy out there knows what I mean when I say, Sometimes you meet a woman and your insides just kinda do multiple somersaults. Maybe it's pheromones, maybe it's just pure physical beauty, maybe it's the brain, or maybe it's a healthy mix of all three. Jane was that person to me, and the more I got to know her, the more she kept getting under my skin. Highly intelligent, well educated, incredibly sexy, loved to party, and adventurous as fuck in every sense of the word. The confidence she exuded in everything she did was palpable whether it was warranted or not, and I was drawn to it.

Jane liked sex, and she liked it a lot. No place was off-limits. We hooked up in taxicabs, at the Metropolitan Opera, on flights, in restaurant bathrooms, on a boat trip with ten other people right around us. The woman was wild in every way imaginable, and satisfied so much of what I wanted in a partner: we would fall into deep, stimulating conversations on a wide array of topics from books to movies to politics; she enjoyed theater as much as I did; our taste in art was the same; she had started to engage in adventure sports and wanted more of it.

She had been clubbing since she was 13 and absolutely loved deep house music, and we would dance all night, high on ecstasy, at underground warehouse clubs in Brooklyn. But I could also take her rock climbing up remote walls of granite, or snowboarding in the backcountry of the Rocky Mountains. There was this one catch though: she was completely nonmonogamous in a way I didn't even know existed, and she had no intention of changing that.

On the surface, her nonmonogamous lifestyle was interesting to me, since the rush of pushing myself to places that both terrify me and take my body to the limits is the fantastic part of life, and fantastic beats the shit out of mundane. That desire for intense experiences drew me deep into the world of extreme sports and it has expressed itself in my sex life too. I've sought out a wide variety of sexual experiences with, well, a wide variety of women.

Those experiences have been exciting, eye-opening, incredibly erotic, and sometimes even downright repulsive. Some were just enjoyably strange, such as when for a few months, in my first apartment after graduating college, I was sleeping with my 45-year-old landlady in lieu of rent. Some were highly charged, like the first time, as a young man, I had an older girlfriend, a professional ballet dancer, who taught me the ins and outs of anal sex, which she preferred to vaginal sex. Some were a "No, that didn't work for me so much," like Dom Daddy/little girl roleplay (you can look it up). Others were an absolute "never again," like some bathroom-level events (no judgment, just wasn't for me). And then there are nights you never forget, such as having a threesome with two stimulating women in a positive and emotionally charged erotic environment, one of whom I was deeply connected to, the other being an object of my desire. Nights like that were, without a doubt, on a par with finishing a hard mountain adventure or standing on the bottom of the ocean without an air tank. Those natural highs are a consequence of my desire to seek out the edge of experience, in places where I was afraid to go, just for the sake of the experience itself.

Before I met Jane, I had dabbled in some form of nontraditional relationship or other for most of my adult life. Previous girlfriends and I would occasionally have other women join us, and sometimes meet up with other couples in a swapping situation. But Jane was different. She thought of that kind of nonmonogamy as beginner mode, or "a good start." She respected it, but she needed something with a lot more intensity, freedom, and edge. As Jane liked to say, she was at the extreme end of the novelty-seeking spectrum. Coupled with her high sex drive, that meant her idea of a nonmonogamous relationship was that she had every intention of sleeping with whoever she wanted to, whenever she wanted to.

Excerpt from Jane's blog:
There is some fuckwit's article in the *Huffington Post* on the reasons why women shouldn't be having casual sex. Here are her reasons and here are my reasons why I think she's a moron.

Reason 1: Casual sex rarely satisfies female sexual needs *. . . because women only want sex when they are in love. And when single women feel horny, it is "an extension of their emotional need for companionship."*

That is the most patronizing, offensive bullshit I've heard in a long time! How dare you tell me what I want?! I know this may be difficult for someone stuck in the 17th century to understand, but I often need sex as much as (if not more than) I need love. And when I feel horny, it's because I want a big fat cock in my pussy, not arms around my back. And casual sex with someone I find attractive is a great way to satisfy my sexual needs.

What Jane wanted from our connection was way beyond what I had ever thought of as a legitimate relationship model. It was scary, the idea of a completely open relationship that was essentially public for the world to see. As Jane and I got closer, I could feel the fear; I could feel the evolutionary survival instinct kicking in, telling me to run away, it's too dangerous. But the adventure seeker in me was being drawn to her. Drawn to this vibrant woman who stimulated every part of my mind and body in a way nobody else ever had. This was a situation where I knew my assumptions were going to be tested, and my ability to cope and to be self-aware was going to be challenged in ways I probably couldn't even comprehend.

In deciding to move forward into a relationship and then marriage with Jane, I turned to my experiences in the world of extreme sports to help me through. I found out that they weren't so different. Yes, one has more physical risk, and the other more emotional risk, but participating in extreme sports at high levels requires the ability to handle powerful emotions, fear first among them. That would prove to come in handy in this open-as-fuck relationship I was being drawn into. It was just a question of training myself to have the kind of mental and emotional awareness I would need on this new terrain. The beauty being that in both areas, the lasting results, the impact of the experience, correlates directly to the amount of effort put in and the risk taken.

It goes without saying that if you want to climb sheer rock faces, BASE jump off of cliffs bridges and buildings, snowboard epic remote mountain terrain, or participate in any other kind of extreme sport, you need to spend some time training, learning skills and the environment before setting out. I had never really thought of my romantic relationships in that way, for the simple reason that I hadn't had to. But now here was a woman who was showing me that same tension of fear and excitement in an intimate connection.

I have always appreciated sexually liberated women, and sought out women who proudly flew their freak flag as my partner. But I had a blind spot I was completely unaware of—I sought out these women as long as they conformed to what I deemed was the correct amount of "freakiness." This blind spot was brought to my attention with all the subtlety of a two-by-four to the face as I got deeper into my connection with Jane.

> *Excerpt from Jane's blog:*
> - I'm a total, proud, and unapologetic slut.
> - My definition of a slut: A person who fully embraces her sexuality, whatever that may be and regardless of what others might think about it.
> - I've always been a slut.

- I've had threesomes, foursomes, moresomes, group sex of all kinds.
- I've slept with over 500 people.
- I love adventure sports: rock climbing, snowboarding, surfing. I've even made a skydive.

I imagine if you have picked up this book, you are at least curious about non-monogamy and may be interested in someone else's experience to help you understand your own journey. Please know, I'm definitely not here to preach that it's the right way to live, or to tell you I've figured out some easy secret to being successful at it, and I certainly don't have an advanced degree in psychology or human relationships (though, ironically, Jane does). As far as my professional life goes, I can't say that I'm anything more than above average in terms of success, although if I were fabulously rich from my business acumen, would you listen to me any more intently on this subject?

Honestly, I'm just a guy—a guy who's hopeful he's above average, a guy who frequently wears a tool belt and who's trying to navigate through the world with some semblance of class and grace, a guy who wants to sample all he can of what's on offer during this thing we call life. Or as I like to call this life model, experience hunting.

What I can offer you is my story, which is very real and hard-earned, and whatever perspective I've picked up along the way. My daily struggle is real, my desire for happiness normal. I keep trying to find that perfect balance point on what I call the bland-to-toxic masculinity continuum, with Sensitive New Age Guy on one end and Bro on the other. Neither end of the spectrum appeals to me, hypersensitive and completely harmless on one side, emotionally (and possibly physically) dangerous on the other. Figuring out how to take the best part of both ends of the spectrum seems to be the goal: embracing my strength, and toughness, while allowing my softer side to appear when appropriate.

I've asked myself: "What does it mean to embrace my masculinity?" Part of it is I want to be thought of as the provider —keeping the roof over your head, putting food on the table, the breadwinner, a very gender-normative male vision. I'm all about being the boy.

There is also a part that wants to instill a healthy mix of safety with a slight element of caution in my female counterpart. Safety in that you know I can be a safe space for you, that I'll hold you, that I'll listen and be empathetic to your needs, emotional or physical. Safety in that you know I'm physically strong enough to protect you and that I always will, but with a little caution too, because you recognize that my strength could be used in unvirtuous ways if I were less of a man. The term *Fierce Gentleman* seems to encapsulate all of the above and the exact, elusive balance point on the continuum for me, so I've chosen to adopt it to direct my own ambitions as to who I want to show up as.

My life and "career," if you can call it that, have been incredibly varied. I've started businesses and closed them after they failed. I've worked on Wall Street because I wanted to make a lot of money and then left it because it kinda sucked and was filled with soulless individuals. I lived out of my truck for a couple of years, and dumpster-dived for food at times. I've won a bronze medal in an extreme sport at the national level, renovated several houses with my own hands, and traveled to every state in the Union. I've had chlamydia and crabs (but not at the same time), jumped out of airplanes thousands of times, and coauthored, with Jane, a lengthy article published in *Cosmopolitan* about what happens at a high-end New York City sex party, under the byline Anonymous.

I've said things I wished I hadn't, and behaved in ways I wished I hadn't. I've tried to make it as a photographer and failed, tried to make it as a writer and failed (obviously), tried to play a musical instrument with some level of proficiency and failed. I've surfed waves that terrified me, taught college-level physics, played in dad-bod sports leagues after miserably failing to become a pro athlete, read a lot of books, dated women twenty-five years older and twenty-five years younger than I was, been swept off a mountain in an avalanche, worked as a biomedical research engineer, done copious amounts of drugs, and made deep, life-enhancing, lasting connections with friends that have stood the test of time, which is the achievement I'm most proud of.

Experience hunting has drawn me to free solo (no ropes) rock climbing, extreme snowboarding where falls have consequences, free diving (no tank) to astonishing depths, midnight skydiving while high as fuck, BASE jumping, bandit bike racing through downtown traffic, and entering into a relationship with Jane, a publicly nonmonogamous, self-described slut and the quintessential party girl of New York City.

A lot of these activities required getting comfortable with risk, as well as getting at least proficient enough in the skills needed to keep the risk manageable. The more dangerous, risky, or precarious the experience, the more intense the emotions that accompany it. And to me, that has always been a major part of the allure, whether the emotions are good, bad, or ugly. The struggles I go through physically to train, and emotionally to keep the anxiety and fear at bay, in order to participate, have made me what I am.

My friends and I refer to this as "Seeking the Risk, Not the Reward," which is a way to make sure your motivations are authentic: Am I seeking out the experience, and all the attendant risks, or do I just want the reward of being able to say I did it? Beyond that, I know if I immerse myself in an experience for the right reasons, then I'll embrace all the effort and all the struggles and all the risks along the way. Over the long run, that approach leaves permanent marks on my soul. That's what I'm searching for, and to me, that's what life is about.

Experience hunting is the opposite of what I call trophy bagging—merely adding notches to one's bedpost for the sake of a number, or to gain an edge in social competition. (Trophy bagging is definitely all about seeking the reward, not the risk.) As a younger man I certainly exhibited more trophy-bagging behavior than I am comfortable admitting. The starkest example of which was a pivotal moment in my late twenties. I was setting out on a big climb with a college buddy, and I was nervous about it because we were taking a route that was not standard and had some significant risk associated with it. As we started the climb, which was going to take several days, I remember wishing it were already over so I could add it to my climbing résumé (a notch on my bedpost). I was shocked when I realized what I was thinking, and it produced an extraordinary moment of clarity. I realized how critical it was for me to understand my motivations, and I fully comprehended the difference between wanting to *do* something hard, versus wanting to be able to *say* that I did something hard.

As I embraced this idea and started to scrutinize my motivations around the extreme sports I engaged in, it bled over into my sex life. I began to see how much I had been driven to accumulate notches on the bedpost because I needed validation from other people that I was a sexually desirable man. Sport fucking, whether you think it's good or bad, is certainly like anything else in that it can be done for the right reasons or the wrong reasons. Too much of my motivation for doing it was coming from the wrong reasons, which meant I wasn't being authentic to myself or to the world. That wasn't the person I wanted to be, and that became of paramount importance to me as I got older.

I didn't stop the casual sex, but I stopped doing it for a number and I stopped telling my friends about it. It was an interesting experiment. If no one was going to know about my exploits, how would it affect the sexual choices I made? To choose to engage or not became purely a matter of self-gratification (and my partner's of course) and nothing more. This seemed a more authentic way to live.

Ladies and Gentlemen, the Bronx Is Burning

When things get too easy or comfortable, I generally make a drastic change in order to stir the pot. I put myself into some sort of stress and conflict, both because life is more interesting to me that way, and stress and conflict produce growth in me in a way that doesn't seem possible with a comfortable existence.

From what I've been able to observe, this principle applies more generally. Take New York City, for example. Back in the 1980s, New York produced some of the greatest artists we have seen in recent history. Jean-Michel Basquiat, Richard Prince, Keith Haring, and Jeff Koons, to name a few. And it's no coincidence, I think, that New York in the 1980s was a scary, dangerous, and crazy place to be. I know this firsthand because I grew up there. Perhaps it was my childhood during this tumultuous time, when there was no shortage of adventure and fear on the streets, that shaped my desire to seek out the ragged edge of experience.

I exhibited experience-hunting characteristics from an early age, or to read that another way, I was probably a fairly typical ADD 13-year-old boy living in a dynamic environment. My upbringing as the only child of liberal parents in rough-and-tumble New York definitely helped instill in me the idea that seeking risk, adventure, and knowledge is what made my life rich. My parents were both born here as well—my mom is from the Bronx and my dad from Brooklyn. They still live here and will most likely die here, both of them lifers in a city that has had its ups and downs during their time.

By all accounts, the 1960s and 1970s were not good to New York City, but my parents and their friends refused to follow the great white flight out to the suburbs. Instead, they stayed put, enrolling their kids in public school and entrenching themselves in the fabric and culture of what was a city in turmoil. They put up with the crime and rotting infrastructure because the theater, the arts, and the museums were the point for them. That's who my role models were growing up, pushing through the shit because there was gold underneath if you knew where to look. It's because of people like them, who stuck with New York and understood what the city was and why it was a great place to live, that we even have a city worth living in today.

My mom was a lifelong public-school teacher in an impoverished neighborhood in the South Bronx and was part of the first teachers' strike in 1968. The neighborhood she taught in became increasingly depopulated and desolate in the 1970s and early '80s, a casualty of deindustrialization and the city's economic collapse. These were the years when landlords torched empty buildings for the insurance money and left blocks of rubble in their wake (look up "the Bronx is burning" online—the pictures will blow your mind). During that period, cops started calling the precinct by her school Fort Apache, and the nickname spread when a movie about the precinct called *Fort Apache, the Bronx* came out in 1981 (residents of the area were less happy with the implications of the name, and protested the movie).

After finishing film school in the early '60s, my father, a beatnik folk singer, came back to NYC to try to make it as a musician. He sang in the various Greenwich Village music venues, such as Cafe Wha, the Bitter End, and Gerde's Folk City, and rubbed elbows and performed with many of the greats, Bob Dylan, Joan Baez, Joni Mitchell, and Pete Seeger, to name a few. When he met my mother, he abandoned his struggling music career and started a small film company whose biggest claim to almost fame was creating and producing the public service spot for the NYPD to help catch David Berkowitz, better known as the Son of Sam serial killer, in 1977. Berkowitz was apprehended the day before the release of the PSA.

My parents were not the overbearing kind, and by the time I was 13, I had the run of the city. I learned to love the adventure that NYC had to offer me and I was drawn to the funky and artistic, albeit rougher, neighborhoods. I know a lot of people romanticize that period, when the artistic scene was on fire, but the reality was that the city was overrun with crime and garbage, and I had my fair share of brushes with violence. Hanging out in the East Village, aka Alphabet City, had its wonderful moments but also plenty of close calls—on one memorable occasion a friend got a bottle broken over his head, and on another a different friend was shot (he lived). Either I was a faster runner or just damn lucky that I never had any serious violence imparted on my body. But without a doubt, those risks introduced me to the impact of intense experiences and the emotions that accompany them.

I wanted to feel as alive as I could, and New York City was full of opportunities to feel that way. Going into bad sections of town to buy fireworks or weed. Spending all night in the dark public parks doing who knows what with my friends. Running around on rooftops and jumping across the gaps between buildings. With luck and some street smarts, I managed to come through it all mostly unscathed, and stronger for it.

As I grew older and traveled outside New York, my adventures got bigger. I wanted to experience it all, try everything, and meet everyone. If it was challenging, I wanted to do it. If it was different, I wanted to experience it. If I hadn't been there, I wanted to go there. I was a full-fledged experience hunter, seeking out variety and intensity wherever I could find them.

In my various extreme adventures, I've touched the void and come back, time and again, to a better place. It's what the journey has produced in me that in itself is the prize—the changes that are forever imprinted on my person. I learned from seeing the effect that my adventures had on me, whether they were successful or not, that I must seek the risk not the reward.

I now try to apply this principle to every area of my life—I want to always find the courage to run toward the burning building. Sometimes I'm doing just that even though the interaction might seem completely ordinary from the outside. While still in the courtship period with Jane, one evening we went to a fancy downtown party where there were lots of well-dressed and put-together socialites. I walked into the main room and saw a few groups to talk to, and then I saw a gentleman standing on his own who was very disheveled and physically unappealing.

It's at moments like this when all the shit of growing up comes crashing back into the forefront of my consciousness. Part of my brain sends me back to being a child at the playground, with an image, accurate or not, of being a slight, geeky redhead who was teased relentlessly. There I was at a chic party with a group of superhip-looking socialites and a woman who I was hoping to impress, and that one glimpse of an "uncool" person brought back that old, old feeling, front and center, that perhaps I didn't belong either.

We know there is a pecking order to social situations whether we choose to pay attention to it or not, and I'm not embarrassed to admit that my initial reaction was to avoid the "unpopular" guy for fear of being associated with him. It was the playground all over again. When that formative-years shit starts bouncing around my head, it's almost inevitable that fear will start to arise. This is when all the extreme-sports experience kicks in and I become acutely aware of the emotion. Rather than being a slave to fear, it triggers my experience hunting philosophy, and my aversion to engaging with him was exactly the thing that motivated me to approach him.

By this point in my life, I understood that my preconceived ideas about who he was, as well as my childhood fears of being judged by the room (the playground), were preventing me from living my best life. The push—getting past my fears, taking on the risk, and taking note of my reactions—is precisely the point. The key question I keep returning to is "What am I missing out on because of these fears and a desire to stay in my comfort zone?" The only way I know to answer that question is by making a concerted effort in my life to get comfortable being uncomfortable.

Back at the playground (that is, the stylish downtown party) I ended up having an amazing conversation with the man and learned a lot about living with physical challenges. He had an infectiously inspirational outlook on life, which I assume he had developed as a way to cope with all the difficulties he had been through. Also, without my knowing it at the time, Jane took notice of whom I chose to engage with, which leveled me up in her eyes —the exact opposite of what my irrational fears were telling me would happen.

So, I would like to tell you a story about how deep I got into the non-monogamy world with Jane, who pushed me to go way beyond my comfort zone in a lot of different ways. As I bare to you all of my insecurities, many failures and embarrassments, and some rather intimate moments in my life, you should know that sharing these things has been no easy task for me, and I think I have that in common with a lot of men.

Oddly, one of the reasons I have written this narrative is to try to learn how to be more grounded with who I am, and to be vulnerable about the things that I'm uncomfortable admitting. Here too, I'm outside my comfort zone, and that's why I can't walk away. So just telling my story is no doubt taking some work here, and your involvement as the reader has now made you complicit in my journey for a more authentically lived life. I thank you for that.

As you read, I hope you will see that I decided to take on the challenge of this relationship with Jane, one that certainly put me in harm's way emotionally, because life had already shown me that even if the relationship failed miserably, which I felt it probably would, there was a very good chance I would come out the other side a fantastically better version of myself.

Chapter 2
The Disruptions Are Where True Living Begins

There are those hard moments in a lifetime of moments that you keep coming back to over and over again, thinking, If I could just change this one tiny thing, the world I inhabit would be completely different. One of those moments was when I asked Tommy, my housemate and one of my closest friends at the time, if I could use his truck. It was such a simple request.

A few years earlier, I had taken advantage of the rampant mortgage opportunities of the mid-2000s and used just about every penny of savings I had to cover the down payment and materials to renovate a historic but rundown multifamily townhome in Manhattan. I had gotten to know Tommy from the competitive skydiving world. He was a contractor, so I hired him to help me tear the place apart and put it back together. Working on a shoestring budget, I lived in the building as we were renovating it, while at the same time I was trying to hold down a regular job as a programmer on Wall Street. After I ran out of money, Tommy offered to continue working on the project if he could live there rent-free for the foreseeable future. I enthusiastically agreed and what was already a good friendship just got deeper.

For a couple of years, we lived and breathed renovations as well as wild and crazy fun, and I think back to that time with such happiness. We were young and dumb and the city was our playground. Many a night we would ride our bikes downtown to the East Village, get completely fucked up on cocktails and cocaine, and then race each other in the traffic back uptown on First Avenue at 3 a.m. Yeah, not the smartest, but fun, and it helped burn off some of the alcohol and drugs before bed.

The *New York Post* even did a full-page spread on a nighttime BASE jumping adventure we did off of Riverside Church, where I was working ground crew and acting as the handler for the reporters while Tommy jumped. On more than one occasion we had a fun MFM threesome in the construction zone that we were living in. Something about men in tool belts really worked to our advantage. We were wild together, although to be fair I always thought he was far crazier than I was. Of course, I lived life on the edge, too, but I was in control, unlike Tommy. (There is that timeless bit of wisdom from George Carlin: "Everyone who drives slower than I do is an idiot, and everyone who drives faster than I do is a maniac.")

One Friday morning I asked if I could borrow the truck to head up to the Shawangunk Mountains for a weekend of rock climbing and skydiving. He said he was planning on using it to go BASE jumping that weekend out in Pennsylvania, but since the weather was good, he could take his motorcycle instead, so I could use the truck.

A short time later I got the call that he had wrecked on the FDR Drive going a hundred miles per hour. He lived through the crash but slowly died over the next three weeks, which was brutal to watch. The last time I saw him alive he was in a hospital bed, unable to talk, and struggling to breathe, but his eyes focused on mine when I walked in the room and I saw the panic in them. He knew the end was near. He died two days later.

Through Tommy's death I came to understand how valuable, and how fragile, the relationships in my life are, which allowed me to feel wealthy in a way I had never considered. It's not like I didn't value my relationships before losing him. I had formed many deep friendships in my life, starting with my first-grade pals, whom I am still incredibly close to, and adding a few more in high school and college. Then I formed a tight group of friends when I was full-time in the adventure sports world.

I know there must have been a part of me that always valued deep connections, especially those that challenged me or could open my eyes to other perspectives. But in losing someone so close to me, I realized I had been taking a lot about those connections for granted. I started to see how much work and effort my friends and I had put into them, and how much better they certainly made my life. I knew my friends felt the same way.

I was in my thirties when Tommy died, and the cataclysmic shock turned my world upside down. "Relationships above all else" was how I was going to live my life from that point forward. But by "relationships," I was referring only to friendships, as I still hadn't gotten a grasp on what a lifetime romantic partner would look like. Interestingly, Jane told me at one point that one of the things that attracted her to me was my ability to maintain such great long-term friendships.

Just When I Had Life All Figured Out

In my twenties, I pursued intense experiences not only for themselves but also, I'm embarrassed to admit, because they seemed to impress my peers. Given that I had a highly active sex drive, impressing women was of paramount importance to me. I cared about the way other people perceived me, both women and men, and sexual prowess was a big part of that. The more women who wanted me, the better I felt, so naturally, I tried to have sex with the greatest number of women possible. Yes, the sex was fun and exciting, but much of it was pursued because I hoped to boost my image among my friends. Total trophy-bagging behavior.

But as I entered my thirties, the lessons I had learned from climbing mountains—about seeking the experience rather than the notch on the bedpost—helped me understand my motivations in other parts of my life. I began to look at my interactions from a new angle: What if I established *my own* identity, set my own standards, rather than allow the rest of the world to do it for me? Could I do it? Could I get to a point where the way other people saw me mattered less? Could this mean I was actually starting to grow up? Was I becoming a fully baked adult at what I considered to be the incredibly experienced age of 35? I felt so goddamn mature.

As I moved into my late thirties, it was remarkable how sure I was that I had this life thing all figured out. I was seeking the risk more often than the reward and feeling like I was presenting my authentic self to the world. I had come to understand the value of the deep friendships that I had cultivated in my life, and I was deliberately living in a way that continued to cultivate them. I was still working on Wall Street, but now for myself, and also feeling good about a number of other professional endeavors that had panned out well. I was having lots of great sex with a variety of women and walking into most situations feeling like "I got this." I was arrogant and I was naive enough to believe in my own arrogance. But my lifelong pattern has been that as soon as things get too comfortable, too easy, whether actually easy or not, I get bored. That's when it's time to burn the house down.

> *Excerpt from Jane's blog:*
> That one time I didn't have sex on the first date was the first and last time I intentionally tried that. It's just not for me. I like to have sex right away, I need to know sex works before I start making life plans with whoever he is, and I need to know that he wants to date a woman who would have sex right away (otherwise he's not the right partner for me).

I met Jane in my apartment of all places. I had been in a somewhat "flexible" relationship with Sylvie, my girlfriend of three years, and it was with her that I had my first foray into true consensual non-monogamy. Through a website, Sylvie and I had met another like-minded couple, and we had a few fun swinging experiences with them. Over the year we knew them, they were becoming more than just sex partners, but actual friends, and we started seeing them socially as well. Right at the time we met them, I had started renovating an apartment and then spent the next year totally gutting and rebuilding it on nights and weekends.

Sylvie and I were living in the apartment during the renovations, and when I had finished the majority of the work, and the place was ready for guests, we invited this couple over for dinner. It was that night my life took the turn it did. They brought a woman along with them that they had picked up in a club two months earlier and were having regular threesomes with. It was Jane. She was from Eastern Europe and was now a grad student at an Ivy League school. Tall, slender with broad shoulders, and very sexy. She had a sultry style made all the more impactful by her noticeable accent. Long, straight brown hair, bright brown eyes, and no makeup at all. Every finger on her hands was covered with large silver rings. Nothing about her suggested expensive tastes, just an overabundance of classy confidence and, yes, some serious arrogance too.

Over the course of the (very casual) dinner party, I was completely struck by her. We engaged intellectually, with a dynamic cadence to our conversation I rarely find, and on top of that, she checked almost all the superficial style and physical boxes that I desired in a woman.

Act I, Scene 1

Everyone gets up from the dinner table and the three guests start gathering their things. Adam helps Jane with her coat while the other people are chatting and laughing.

JANE: Hey, thanks for having us over for dinner. That was really fun.

ADAM: Yeah, it was, and it was really nice to meet you.

JANE: Me too, It's always great to show up in a new city and be able to get to know people in a more intimate environment.

ADAM: Look, I know you live outside the city but the next time you're down, my girlfriend and I would love to take you out one night.

JANE: That sounds great if you guys are doing something cultural, or having people over, but I'm sorry to report that I'm not really attracted to your girlfriend so . . .

ADAM: Understood. Till the next time our paths cross then.

At that point in my non-monogamy journey, my girlfriend and I only played together with other lovers, so a physical connection between Jane and me was not to be—yet. But over the next couple of years, Sylvie and I broke up, and became close friends. Meanwhile, Jane and I were slowly becoming friendly in the New York City clubbing scene, where she was making a reputation for herself as the quintessential party girl—and appeared to have a sexual appetite like none I had ever seen before in a woman.

During this period, we had a fun hookup or two. The first time was one of those moments when the stars align perfectly for what was just pure awesomeness. I had a new girlfriend, Nell. Our relationship was nonmonogamous in the same sort of way I was familiar with: we occasionally had women join us in the bedroom as a third.

Nell and I were at this loft party one evening with a bunch of people I knew, including Jane, generally having a good time, when a decision was made to make a move to a new location. As Nell, Jane, and I were headed outside, Jane asked if she could grab a cab ride with us to the new spot.

Piling into the back of the taxi, I ended up in the middle, between the two women. We were all a little buzzed for sure, and having some erotic, flirtatious conversation when Jane asked Nell if she (Jane) could suck my cock right there in the car. Nell was totally supportive of this but only if she could help, so Jane casually unzipped my pants, and the two of them took turns on me as my eyes opened wide and took in the Manhattan skyline that was flying past us. I came in Jane's mouth as I looked into

Nell's eyes while she was kissing me. I have no idea if the taxi driver saw anything or even cared. When we got home later that evening, Nell and I fucked with an intensity we had not experienced with each other before.

So yeah, that taxicab ride was a wonderful introduction to exactly how sexually forward Jane was. It rocked my world and I wanted more. But I was going to have to wait another year till that would happen. By that time, I was no longer with Nell, who had left me for Jesus. It seems my desire for a crazy lifestyle had been the catalyst for her move back to the religious upbringing of her youth. I couldn't tell if she was consciously shaming me but regardless, it certainly hurt a bit. In fairness to her, she did ask me to come along but I said that joining a church and believing in God weren't really in the wheelhouse of an atheist. I think the exact words I used were, "The Lord and I don't see eye to eye on a great number of things."

Relatively newly single, I got invited to a weekend at a friend's mountain retreat with a big group of people. A little dejected that my girlfriend had left me for a guy who died two thousand years ago, I wasn't feeling too motivated to head out of town for the festivities, but my friend, knowing of my attraction to Jane, told me she was going to be there, so I went.

It was a beautiful spot, fifteen miles from the nearest paved road, deep in the heart of the Adirondack Mountains of upstate New York. The cabins were clustered around the property's own private lake. Given that I was a fairly strong swimmer, I decided to swim to a dock on a small island on the other side of the lake and back, probably about half a mile total.

As I was on the return journey, I noticed someone swimming toward me. We met in the middle of the lake, and I was surprised to see that it was Jane. We treaded water for a minute, and she told me that she wanted to swim to the other side but didn't feel strong enough to be able to swim back and asked if I would come get her in the small motorboat parked at the main dock. I grabbed the boat when I got back, shot across the lake, and pulled up to the small dock where Jane was sunning herself in her bikini. She motioned me to come join her on the dock, so I tied up the boat and lay down next to her. She rolled over, half on me, and started rubbing my chest and body.

"I really want to thank you for coming to get me," she said. Then, sliding her hand down my swimsuit, she took out my cock, and we had a fantastic sexual reconnection right on the rough wooden dock on the far side of the lake. Somehow neither of us got splinters in our bare asses. This woman's sexual forwardness was impressive, and I was just getting more and more turned on by it.

The next morning in my cabin I awoke at my normal early hour, threw on a sweatshirt, and walked out to the main building where the kitchen was to make some coffee. I figured I'd be the only one up for a while. I'd sit by the dining room window and look out at the lake with my fresh coffee and something to read. There was no lack of ten- to twenty-year-old copies of *Time*, *Life*, and the odd hunting magazine strewn around the old lodge.

As the coffee was brewing, Jane walked into the kitchen. She grabbed the pot and poured us a couple of mugs and was particularly impressed that as an American I drank my coffee black, as she did. Lucky for me, I had only started doing it a couple months earlier.

We walked into the rustic dining room and sat down at a small table by the window overlooking the lake. A loose mist hanging over the water, the morning light, our mugs of coffee in hand, it was a departure from the environment in which we had been getting to know each other over the past couple of years.

I knew Jane was from Eastern Europe, but not much more than that. As we warmed up into our conversation, she started to tell me stories from her youth. What it was like growing up under a benevolent dictator in socialist Yugoslavia, where no one had a lot, but everyone had enough. How overwhelmed with choice she was when she first came to the United States. Until she walked into an American supermarket—on a visit at the age of 14—she had had no idea that there were that many types of breakfast cereal. When she was 8, her parents divorced. She told me about how her dad waged a bitter custody battle over her, which he ultimately won, resulting in her estrangement from her mother. Unfortunately, he had no real interest in doing the work to actually raise a child and had only fought so hard for Jane to hurt her mom.

She also told me about the dark side of her youth after Yugoslavia fell apart. During the transition to democracy, the normal rules that society puts in place to keep kids safe weren't there. No one carded a minor for anything, cigarettes, alcohol, or entrance to nightclubs. In that sort of environment, and with little parental supervision, she grew up fast and got herself into all sorts of trouble as an early teen. She learned that she could only rely on herself to keep herself safe.

As bad as her father was as a primary caregiver, he did instill in her a love of science and knowledge, and was a tireless teacher to her. She was a straight-A student throughout high school. Seeing the free-and-easy lifestyle he enjoyed as a university professor, she decided early on that academia was for her. She also knew it was her best ticket out of Eastern Europe.

She attended the local university, studying psychology, and spent six months of her senior year in Berlin. She told me all about the free-spirited bohemian scene she was immersed in there: electronic music, art, culture, drugs, partying, and, of course, wild sexual experiences.

We had a good time comparing notes on the New York City of the '80s I had known and her experience in a unified Berlin, which seemed similar in a lot of ways. She couldn't stop asking me questions about my years growing up in the city, and what it was like back then. I told her about all the adventures I'd had, the street art of the time, and seeing the effects of a city in transition. She held a certain nostalgia for what I was describing, and I countered with the realities of what daily life was like for so many people during that period, the crack and AIDS epidemics raging, and a large percentage of the city's population living in poverty.

This debate turned into a philosophical discussion on whether it was possible to create an urban environment with artistic freedom, wildness, and vibrancy that was also well-functioning and safe. Perhaps the anarchic quality of urban life that we appreciated was a consequence of the breakdown of the social fabric and infrastructure—and all the hazards that entailed for people without the means and resources we had.

One of Jane's lifelong dreams was to live in NYC, something that had become closer to a reality when she started her PhD program not far from the city. I filed that nugget of information away in my brain.

Our solitude was eventually broken when the other adult campers started to wake up. People wandered into the kitchen and dining room and there was a move to make breakfast. The rest of the day was spent on group hikes through the woods to waterfalls and lookout points. Along the way, we continued our conversation. We talked about religion and science—both of us were atheists—and spent a long while discussing the historical conflict between them. She was taught from a very early age in the public schools of Yugoslavia that religion was a thing of the past since we now had science, and that no one educated still believed in it. She had quite the shock waiting for her on that account when she got to the United States.

We also spent a lot of the weekend exploring the ways our bodies fit together, in the woods, by the lake, on the docks, and in the rustic buildings that dotted the property. I have this great memory of a wild thunderstorm raging while we were fucking the shit out of each other in her cabin. The buildings only had twin beds, so there wasn't a lot of space to work with. Jane was on her stomach, one hand grabbing the metal of the bed frame, the other rubbing her clit, causing her to come over and over again. Her back was slightly arched so her perfect ass was raised up toward me as I was rhythmically moving in and out of her from my push-up position. I was losing my mind contemplating how hot her body was from the back, framed on the small summer-camp-style bed with the loose, thin white sheet sliding around on the dingy, old mattress. The rain was pelting the window in front of us and the nonstop thunderclaps were deafening. The energy of our connection seemed to be in accord with what the weather gods were dishing out.

I don't know how many times we physically connected over the course of those three days, but it was a lot. After all that conversation, all that connection, all that sex, I desired more of her, and she could tell. But this was not something she was ready for, or even wanted for that matter, so when we parted at the end of that weekend, she gave me a warning: "Now, don't you fall for me. I'm not the kind of girl who has a boyfriend."

The words landed pretty hard. After an idyllic weekend like that, she was saying that's as far as it would go. I couldn't understand why, as it seemed we meshed with each other in such a good way. A way that I hadn't with anyone else I'd met before, much less hooked up with, and hooked up with very well. From the dynamic discussions we'd had, to silly little things like we both put only olive oil and balsamic vinegar on salad, and disliked mushrooms.

We parted ways after the weekend, but I was not content to accept her statement. After two months of my trying to figure out how to orchestrate a "coincidental" meet up, out of dumb luck, one of my oldest best friends from first grade was having a wedding just a few miles from her university. It was perfect. I could reach out without it seeming like I was chasing her down. I just happened to be in the neighborhood.

The day after the wedding, Jane and I met for coffee in the afternoon and spent a couple hours catching up. I asked her about her doctoral work in psychology. She told me about a study she was conducting on how casual sex affects mental health (go figure), and about a new sexual orientation they were just identifying, "mostly straight." It described individuals who weren't completely straight, but weren't same-sex oriented enough to see themselves (or be seen by others) as fully bisexual.

She asked me about the new tech business I had started, located out west in Colorado, which was fast becoming a tech hub. I talked about how we were building affordable tech to help small restaurants compete online with large chains without having to be a slave to the Grubhub and Seamless giants of the world, something she appreciated. We were, I said, trying to secure several million in funding to grow faster and it was proving to be quite a lesson in how to sell yourself, and your ideas.

We talked about a recent skydive she had made, which was particularly interesting to me. I loved how emotionally aroused she got as she talked about the jump, as well as the skiing and snowboarding she had done in Europe.

It was a PG-rated afternoon in the coffee shop, and when we finished our drinks, I assumed we would say goodbye. Jane, however, had other things in mind. She suggested we go over to her friend's car parked in the adjacent lot and fuck. It was totally in broad daylight, with people everywhere, which I was definitely uncomfortable about, but agreed without hesitation. Jammed into the back seat of a Ford Festiva, I was lying down in the back seat with her on top of me and no room to maneuver, but she managed to ride me well enough to bring us both to orgasm within minutes. I was *really* enjoying every aspect of this woman.

With our friendship developing via consistent online chatting, and me being the schemer that I am, knowing that she had a desire to explore climbing, I took a mutual friend out on the rocks one day knowing full well he would post of pictures of the adventure on social media. About a day later, she reached out to ask if I would take her rock climbing. The hook was in and as far as she was concerned it was all her idea.

We made plans to do just that a few weeks later and lucky for us it was a gorgeous fall Thursday in the Shawangunk Mountains, about ninety minutes north of the city. We spent the day having a few adventures on the rocks, and this woman took to climbing in a way I had never seen before in a novice. She seemed to have no fear, which was incredibly attractive.

We were supposed to climb for only two days, but she wanted more and we spent four days up there, climbing in the mornings and spending the afternoons drinking coffee and co-working in the house we were staying at. It was my friend's place, a new, supermodern post-and-beam house he had built right near the cliffs. There was a moment when I just had to pause and take a look at where I was and what was happening. Sitting and working at this large wooden table, situated in this light-flooded, massive barn-style room with 35-foot ceilings, gorgeous large, blonde wooden beams crisscrossing the space above us, the house surrounded by forest, with the Wallkill River snaking right by the property, and the cliffs visible off in the distance. And sitting across from me, quietly working away on her research, was Jane, a woman whom I had been climbing with all morning, with whom the sex was mind-blowing, who was at the very least my intellectual equal but probably way more than that, and who saw the world the same way I did. Jane, who wanted more from life than just existence, who saw the value in seeking the risk not the reward, who fell so easily into this routine with me of fucking, climbing, working, cooking dinner, watching a movie, or just reading the evening away. At that moment it felt like I had found my future.

The long weekend together had the desired effect of pulling us closer together, and at the end of it, she asked if I would accompany her to a professional conference the following month in Puerto Vallarta, Mexico, where we could scuba dive and play in the ocean when she wasn't attending sessions. This scheme of getting her to make the moves was starting to work better than I had planned, and my years of engaging in adventure sports was paying off in a way I hadn't anticipated. I accepted her invitation.

I knew a great little surf town about an hour north of where the conference was, and I told her I might hang there during the peak of her conference responsibilities, once again dangling the hook. Her taste for adventure (and adventure sports) being what it was, she ended up staying up there with me for a few nights and missed part of the conference so I could teach her to surf.

Despite her best efforts, this was starting to become a relationship of sorts, as it was apparent we were connecting on so many levels. We would spend long mornings drinking coffee and debating which was better, the self-governance of western democracy versus the benevolent dictator model that she had grown up with. Her experience taught her that socialist life was safer and easier. After Yugoslavia's collapse, the safety and security that she had enjoyed as a child was gone, and before long its member states had descended into a series of ugly interethnic wars. It's true that she took advantage of the freedoms that came with the chaos that ensued, but she recognizes now that it was not a healthy way for her to grow up.

This led her to believe that the general public was too stupid to be able to pick their own leaders and that the benevolent dictator was a far more successful model.

I countered by asking, "How can you be sure that the dictator will always be benevolent?"

"You can't, of course, and that's the danger of giving one person too much power," she conceded. "But consider this: twenty years after Yugoslavia dissolved, over eighty percent of ex-Yugoslavians believed that life was better under Tito."

I don't know how many hours we spent on this particular topic, but sheesh, this woman could debate passionately and we both vibed on it.

Act I, Scene 23

It's the end of Adam and Jane's week together in Mexico. They sit next to each other in beach chairs, watching the sun set over the water. They have just been served margaritas and they are the only ones on the beach. The waves are the only sound until Jane breaks their silence with a warning.

JANE: If we're going to be spending time together, you need to know that I sleep with a lot of other men and women, and that's not going to change.

ADAM: I understand. Just out of curiosity, how many people do you think you've slept with?

JANE: Somewhere between four and five hundred.

(Long pause.)

ADAM: Okay, that's significantly more than I've been with and I thought I'd been with a lot.

JANE: How many?

ADAM: I stopped counting about ten years ago but around a hundred, I'm guessing.

JANE: That's not bad.

ADAM: And that's definitely not the reaction I normally get when a woman I'm involved with finds that out.

JANE: Yeah, well, I'm not your normal woman.

ADAM: I noticed. What's the craziest thing you've ever done sexually.

JANE: Hmm . . . I'm slightly nervous about telling you, which is not something I would normally feel.

ADAM: I'll take that as a compliment but please, do tell.

JANE: I once got gangbanged and bukkakied by twelve men.

ADAM: No shit.

JANE: No shit.

(Adam takes a healthy sip of his margarita.)

The extent of Jane's wildness was something I wasn't expecting. Not that I was judging her for her choices, but I was starting to wonder if her subtle warning of "be careful what you wish for" was becoming prophetic. All the same, I was becoming deeply attracted to who this woman was as a person, and I wanted more of her.

In all of my previous relationships, I had been the wild man who had to tame it down to my partner's level of adventurousness, be it in sex, social activities, or outdoor adventures. My previous girlfriends were far from passive, and were edgy in their own right, but I was always the one pushing the sexual envelope, curious about connecting with other singles and couples for erotic adventures.

A number of times this led to conflicts in which my partner shamed me for my desires, or perhaps it was just the way I went about discussing them. Subtlety was not my strong suit as a young man.

Early on in my sexual history, I had had a few threesomes. One of my first climbing partners asked me to help him fuck his girlfriend one evening, which was an amazing experience, since at the time she was one of the most sexually desirable women I had ever met. And in college I had been lucky enough to connect with a few women who as a pair liked taking a boy home for the evening. I enjoyed these experiences and sought them out.

As I got further into serious relationships out of college, I was curious about the world of what I thought of at the time as "kinky" sex. Although armed with the knowledge I have now, it was really just group sex: threesomes and foursomes.

To be honest, being a straight male, I've always preferred threesomes with two women, but when I had that early MFM threesome with my climbing buddy, I learned that having another man in the bedroom wasn't threatening to me. Perhaps it was the fact that I was the "other man" in that scenario. I'm guessing that experience made it a lot easier for me when I started crossing that boundary with my girlfriends, and I never seemed to have a lot of jealousy around it. I wasn't turned on by it, but I wasn't turned off by it either. It was just good, clean fun.

So before meeting Jane, I'd had a certain amount of experience with some form of non-monogamy, but I kept that aspect of my relationships a secret from just about everyone else. My non-open (i.e., vanilla) friends and family had no idea. The girlfriends in question liked to keep it that way, too, and I was right on board with it. I was, for lack of a better term, in the closet.

I told myself that a couple's sexuality is a private thing and there's no need to flaunt it, which I do feel is true, but it's not the whole story. The truth is that I was uneasy about being public about my non-monogamy for a couple of reasons. I didn't want to open myself up to questions, to having to defend myself to people who I perceived as not understanding, and, I'm sad to say, the more important reason was the very real possibility of losing respect from the general public, who would ask the question: "What kind of man has a girlfriend who has sex with other men?"

As I've mentioned, I'd already grown up a great deal, moving away from trophy-bagging behavior, and learning to look to myself for my self-worth, rather than to how the general public perceived me. But as far as I'd come, meeting and getting involved with Jane was showing me there was much more terrain ahead that I didn't know how to navigate. I was still stuck in this place of needing second-party validation about my romantic partner, and the judgment that would come with the public knowledge that my partner was a sexually open individual, who allowed other men into her body, was more than I wanted to handle.

> *Excerpt from Jane's blog:*
> I have a lot of casual sex. We're talking about thousands of encounters with hundreds of partners, and I absolutely love it.
>
> The vast majority of my hookups have been pleasurable, some were absolutely mind-blowing,

some were crappy, and a couple bordered on abusive.

With the exception of the borderline abusive ones, all my hookups have left me feeling good about myself and what I had done.

Being public about the nonmonogamous part of my relationships was a scary proposition. I had no desire to shine a spotlight on a relationship configuration that most people would consider to be lifted from a movie plot or cultish behavior. Therefore, in a shroud of sexual privacy is where my girlfriends and I stayed, and at the nonmonogamous limit of what I considered acceptable.

This had been all well and good, but I was quickly realizing that if I wanted to be with Jane, I was going to face some terrifying challenges. Not only was I going to have to be public about our open relationship, but up to this point, my nonmonogamy experiences had all been within the context of having sexual experiences *with* my partner and other individuals and couples. Here was Jane telling me that the only relationship configuration she would engage in was one where, in addition to us playing together, she (and I) could go off on our own and have sex with other people as well. That was certainly different and something I hadn't considered before. At the time, I couldn't even conceive of a completely open relationship as a long-term model. It was, I thought, just where she was at this point in her life, and it would probably change as we got closer. Nevertheless, it was still way out of my comfort zone, and getting into the type of relationship she wanted was scary. But again, scary is attractive to me (up to a point, anyway).

I do recognize the very real truth that I was infatuated with Jane. I was wide eyed over all that she represented in the sexual arena, and all that I saw as available to me with her. She was a doorway into an exciting, scary world where I could live out any of my wildest fantasies. That idea was compelling, so much so that it's possible I was attracted to the idea of her as much as I was to the actual woman.

There is a part of me that wants to say that I was being dragged into a situation that I felt I had no control over, but that's not accurate. I could have stopped the slide anytime I wanted to. I was just so curious about this woman, and so impressed by the depth of my attraction to her. This was a woman who frequently brought me a book as a present when we got together, such a clear sign that someone not only likes you but respects you intellectually. This was a woman who could walk around New York City with me for hours analyzing street art in abstract terms. This was a woman who could explain deep, and sometimes not so deep, theories in psychology to me. This was a woman who liked to fuck the way I liked to fuck, and had a brazenness about her sexuality that was exciting, albeit a bit intimidating. It seemed to have the potential to be a match like no other I'd had before.

So here was the woman I was falling for, and the situation I was falling into, without any idea of what I was doing. Her sexual exploits were common knowledge in the NYC nightlife party scene, but that's not the world I live in most of the time. It's where I engage in fun, wild behavior to relax and shake off the stress. It was a world that the people who made up my everyday reality, my close friends and family, knew nothing about. But you didn't have to be a rocket scientist to figure out that I was getting closer and closer to the inevitable train wreck of one side of my life spilling into the other.

Course Set, Collision Inevitable

As I gradually introduced Jane to my friends and family, they instantly accepted her. How could they not? She was a PhD candidate at a prestigious university, strikingly attractive, and exceptionally outgoing and engaging. She spoke five languages and could intelligently converse with most anyone on a wide variety of subjects. My family couldn't stop talking about her. My friends made social media statements about me running around with European supermodels. Her intelligence and attractiveness played into my need for approval and acceptance, and although I had made real progress along those lines, old habits die hard. With all the authentic attraction I had for Jane, I have to admit I took pleasure in knowing that close friends and family viewed Jane as so desirable. I was—and still am, to some extent—a man with an ego, and that ego fed on validation from the people around me. Validation translated into confidence, confidence translated into success with women, and those two things helped create the self-image I had of myself as a man.

The turning point arrived on the day I got an email from a certain social media platform that read: "Jane has listed herself as being in an open relationship with you. Can you confirm that you are in an open relationship with Jane?"

And there it was: The moment of truth. Late at night, in my apartment, I read that email, and all I could do was stare at it. On the one hand, I was ecstatic that this woman—one whom I respected, enjoyed being with no matter the activity, and on top of it all was having the most amazing sex with—felt close enough to me to be willing to state publicly to the world that we were "an item." On the other hand, it felt like all that second-party validation I had received was going to be gone in an instant. I knew that if I clicked that Confirm button for all the world to see, there would be people who would view me as weak. My sexuality would be front and center for the world to judge. Being honest and transparent seemed like a bridge too far, and I questioned whether I wanted to cross it.

Intellectually, I knew that it's absurd to view a man in an open relationship as weak, but my emotional response was real and powerful. I do not believe that a man whose wife or girlfriend sleeps with other men with the consent of all parties is weak. And yet emotionally, I was plugged into precisely those values.

There I was at a decision point. Did I want to take the easier route, that of a trophy bagger, by moving on to a different partner who could secure for me all the second-party validation I had been enjoying with Jane, but without any of the challenges? Or did I want to take the uncomfortable, scary route of the experience hunter, which would challenge me in ways I had never been challenged before?

True to form, I was drawn to the Confirm button because it made me uncomfortable, and it forced me to face fears that I would have rather not faced. After quite a bit of hesitation, and after telling myself that I was choosing this option with my eyes wide open and that I was clear about what I was signing up for, I clicked Confirm, telling the world that I really liked Jane, that I was in a relationship with her, and that she has sex with other men. I surfed the web for a bit, then went to sleep.

The next morning, I met my cycling team for practice. Not five minutes into the ride, my friend Brian shouted out from the back of the group, "Does anybody know what an open relationship is?" It had begun.

My friends couldn't seem to talk about anything else. It felt like every conversation started with "So, I saw that you're in an open relationship?" My closest friend and climbing partner of twelve years wanted to know, "How can you let other guys fuck your woman?" I had to tell him that there isn't any part of me that believes I "let" her fuck other men any more than I "let" her be female. It's just who she is.

It's curious to me that so many men in contemporary society, apparently myself included, which I was shocked to find out, relate their masculinity to the sexual behavior of their female partners.

Now, I like sex a lot, so I want my partner to like sex a lot. It takes a strong-willed woman to defy society's expectations of what a woman should be, and a woman who flies the flag of her sexuality with pride and authority is no doubt a powerful individual. I'm attracted to powerful women, and I've never understood men who talk about highly sexual women in a negative light. If you're a man who likes sex, it seems counterintuitive and even hypocritical to do so.

> *Excerpt from Jane's blog:*
> Guys, if you want more sexually liberated, open-minded women, treasure her when you find one.

Yet at some level, here I was buying into that way of thinking—a way of thinking that I *knew* I had explicitly and consciously shunned. But in retrospect, I can see that I was only able to do so because I had never met a woman who challenged my idea of what was an acceptable level of sexual expression for my partner.

This all came into laser focus for me during this period of my life, but at no point did I think I had made a mistake. I was enjoying the range of emotions that my choice gave rise to and the personal growth it was cultivating by forcing me to walk the walk, not just talk the talk.

Eventually my friends moved on to other topics. My everyday life remained mostly unchanged, but I did feel different inside. I had faced my fears about what the world would say about me, taken a significant step toward leading a more transparent life, and stood up for the belief in living unapologetically as I chose.

Today, I feel far more powerful than I ever have, and I am no longer guarding a secret. My relationship choices are still the topic of discussion at a dinner party now and again, but for the most part the response is positive, a result of people's curiosity. I enjoy being an advocate for an open way of life, reassuring people that it's okay to like having sex with people other than one's partner.

Choosing to have the relationship with Jane that I did created a unique opportunity for me to begin to understand my own personal shortcomings, and what it means to have authentic masculinity in a way I had never considered. I chose a road that completely smashed some of my existing narratives defining me and my masculinity, which was so scary I don't know if the words I've written can do it justice.

I was facing not only my own fears, but a tremendous amount of disapproval, and a reduction in other people's assessment of my masculinity, sometimes from friends I truly cared about. Had it not been for the deep respect, attraction, and of course infatuation I had for Jane, I might not have chosen that road, but choose it I did. I went to the edge of myself, looked over into the abyss, and decided that growing up meant being confident in my own choices, and accepting my partner's choices. Respect is earned, not given, and to be respected as a man meant behaving in a way worthy of being respected, and not buying into the patriarchal bullshit that, as I found out the hard way, I had been buying into.

This was one of the hardest things I've ever done, and I've done a lot of hard things. The experience I'm about to describe to you is far from perfectly executed or proudly retold, but it certainly illuminated a lot about who I was then and who I am now.

Chapter 3
Wake-Up Call

Excerpt from Jane's blog:
All of you men, who once you get a little taste of me, are then incapable of containing your enthusiasm at how lucky you got to meet someone like me. And so you hungrily want more, you greedily want everything from me, you selfishly want me to become your own personal sex fairy who will magically wave her wand and make all your sex fantasies come true.

You want more, so much more. I'm not talking about a relationship, of course. No, you wouldn't want to date me. I'm way too slutty and wild for your big, manly ego to handle as a girlfriend. No. I'm talking sex. I'm talking every single dark, dirty, taboo sexual fantasy you've ever had. Everything you've been secretly jerking off to for years but were always too scared to admit to your past lovers. Everything your girlfriends, wives, or even casual partners would (or did) balk at, at best, or run kicking and screaming at worst.

I'm flying down Flatbush Avenue at top speed on my bike when a parked car door opens in front of me and my world instantly gets very small. The crazy salad of thoughts that have been swirling around in my head and distracting me instantly disappear and I'm left with one task: don't hit the car door. My only option is to swerve out into the lane of traffic, where my shoulder smashes into the side of a delivery truck that I lean into, trying to become one with it in order to squeeze past the open car door. I'm a pinball in the grinding machine of traffic, with one thought only, keep the rubber side down and all will be okay. I squeak past the car's open door and its surprised occupant, peel off the truck, and continue moving forward, pausing only to throw an elbow backward to get the messenger bag filled with my beach stuff recentered on my back. I'm headed south and making good time toward the Rockaways, a long, sandy peninsula separating Brooklyn from the Atlantic Ocean.

With my focus recovered from the near miss, I stand up and smash down on the pedals, again gripping the handlebars. My teeth are clenched; I'm angry. Who the fuck is this Jane? Her words ring in my ears: "Sweetheart, this is who I am. Did you think I would change?" Well, this is where you wanted to be Adam, pushed out of your comfort zone—but to a level you hadn't anticipated. And now, out on the bike, you're in that euphoric spot where physical exertion, skill, and risk meet. The result of which is identical to what I used to get from dragging razor blades across my skin as an adolescent.

There is nothing like an adrenaline-pumping ride in traffic to calm me down and chill me out. It's the extreme sport of NYC. (Seasoned bike messengers compete against each other in what are called "Alleycats." These are bandit races that run on city streets in full traffic, from one end of the city to the other.) It's full-on aggression between you and the vehicles. Riding at high speed in traffic requires all your focus, since serious injury or death is always lurking only inches away, forcing you to push all your other troubles into the background.

But while I'm trying to focus on the traffic, potholes, and pedestrians, that fucking Jane keeps taking my attention away. I'm gonna get myself killed out here. "Sweetheart, this is who I am. Did you think I would change?" Those words keep floating across my field of vision, obscuring what's in front of me on Flatbush Avenue.

After the dust settled from my big social media coming out, everything was going so well. Over the past year, Jane has been finishing her PhD, and we've been seeing each other about twice a month for a four-day weekend, alternating between the city and the small university town where she lives.

It's been so enjoyable getting closer to her with each visit, and even mundane things, like going to her local supermarket for groceries, take on a vibrant quality. I have this one image of her in tight brown leggings, high-heel boots, and a small furry jacket, sultrily walking down the frozen-food aisle and just thinking how fantastic everything was right then.

It's been great being connected to an academic crowd again and I enjoyed her colleagues' surprise when they found out that Jane had a boyfriend. Our weekends in the city have been filled with cultural events, nightlife extravaganzas, dinner parties, and physical activities. We read to each other in bed, sometimes books, sometimes articles in the paper. I love how irate she gets, yelling about conservatives trying to restrict access to birth control and abortion, or Texas trying to put a high tax on renewable energies to save its fossil fuel industry. Then we'd go at it about the merits of some fiscal policy that either the Republicans or the Democrats were trying to push through. She's far more liberal than I when it comes to economics, so we've had some spirited debates.

I built her a bike and we've been riding all over the city to see strange art shows or street murals in obscure locations or go to new restaurants. We love theater, traditional as well as avant-garde, and make a point of seeing as much as we can. We went snowboarding out west and I even took her ice climbing once. When we're together, we're fully together and having a blast.

I've been satiated in a way I've never been before. Frequently, we fuck four times a day. With regularity we have another woman join us, and occasionally another man, since Jane loves double penetration, and I'm always happy to return the favor when she can find a willing participant. We'd spend our mornings laughing and reliving what took place the night before, whether it had been just the two of us or we'd had a "special guest."

Everything is okay with this woman. Every weird idea that pops into my head can be explored. Even when those things involve boundaries I'm not quite ready to cross, I'm free to be myself about my sex and sexuality without judgment. If it's something that's intriguing enough to be actually explored rather than just talked about, she's fully on board with it. I haven't had to hide my attraction to other women or any of my sexual desires, and there's been such a freedom in that.

In turn, I've been trying to provide the same kind of freedom and acceptance for Jane. With all her previous partners, she had to hide much of who she was sexually. This included Astrid, the woman she considered the love of her life. They had dated and lived together for five years prior to Jane's moving to the United States. Jane tried to open up the relationship several times, but Astrid always insisted that monogamy was the only kind of relationship that expressed true love. Despite how much Jane loved her, she eventually resorted to cheating on Astrid, just as she had cheated on all the others before her. In that relationship, Jane came to understand how much she craved sexual novelty and excitement, something she just couldn't get from a monogamous relationship—no matter how perfect the relationship might otherwise be.

Her rampant infidelity left Jane with feelings of shame and guilt. She didn't want to cheat or lie or hide her sexuality. She didn't want to hurt Astrid, the person she loved the most. The experience taught her that she needed to live openly and freely as who she was. And in New York City, with all its sex-positive spaces and communities, she was finding that it was possible to do just that. I could fully understand how that became a driving force behind her advocacy for consensual non-monogamy.

As we continued to get to know each other over the past year, we've been forging an intense, erotic bond in the bedroom, and out of that sexual intimacy, an emotional connection has been starting to develop. Also, I'm just happier when we're doing things together. It's obvious we have something special, and I've been starting to think that I've finally found someone who I could see myself with for a long time. Yes, we're still relatively new, and not living together, but the signs all indicate we're a good match (or at least all the signs that I had been choosing to look at back then).

All these happy thoughts have me moving on the bike at a much more pedestrian pace. As I get deeper into Brooklyn, I'm passing the rows and rows of classic townhomes that line the streets. The architecture is beautiful and so many have been restored from the devastation that overcame the area in the '70s. Then I begin the climb up to Eastern Parkway, the major dividing line that runs through this area of the borough. Standing up on the pedals, my body swinging back and forth in a rhythmic dance, I imagine myself in the Tour de France, hammering my way up the Alps through some mountain town. But the trees I'm surrounded by aren't the woods of France but Prospect Park, and those flower fields off to my left are the Brooklyn Botanic Garden.

"Sweetheart, this is who I am. Did you think I would change?" I stomp down on the pedals again and the bike lurches forward as I point my head toward a long gap between all the vehicles down the center of the avenue. I'm zipping past the cars on either side of me as if they're standing still. I'm back in the zone.

Have I been lying to myself? Non-monogamy suits me fine, as long as Jane and I are doing it together. But then there's the part I haven't been able handle: That she's been having one-on-one hookups with other men. Up to this point, that aspect of our relationship has been easy for me to ignore since it's been happening up at her school or in the city when I wasn't there, an out of sight, out of mind kind of thing. But Jane's about to finish her doctorate and the plan is that she's going to move in with me. I couldn't be happier. We've even joked about getting married since her student visa is going to run out later this year and it seems like the only option. We've laughed about so much together. I've been so excited about what the future might hold for us, until that moment in her kitchen. We were washing up from dinner.

"I can't wait to move to the city and have so many more men to choose from," she said. "The pickings are getting kind of slim up here."

My brain wasn't sure I had heard that right.

"You plan on keeping this arrangement after we're living together?"

Jane looked at me and said, "How do you mean?"

"Uh . . . can I pass on that question?" I responded.

"Sweetheart, this is who I am. Did you think I would change?"

Reality hit, and it hit hard. Jane's planning to keep on hooking up with other men indefinitely. It shook me to the core how she casually mentioned it in passing, totally oblivious to my thoughts, desires, and expectations.

Wait . . . what?!?!?!?

The best I could do in that moment was to stammer out some response about not having thought much about it, which was sort of true, since I had just assumed that she *would* change, and hadn't really done any processing on the matter. I was in a state of shock. It became obvious to me that I had been comforting myself with a fantasy of what the future would hold with Jane. A fantasy that her behavior was just the result of not having someone she really cared about, and now that we were developing our bond and moving in together, it would start changing. It was all just a dream, and my wake-up call came in right on time to blow my lovely future out of existence. *No, no, no!* I wanted to reject reality and go back to the wonderful dream I'd been having.

I couldn't even truly wrap my brain around what was going on here. She wasn't presenting me with a choice; she was just stating that this was who she was. There was no discussion. Instead, it was our personal version of the old fable about the scorpion and the frog, where the scorpion lets the frog know ahead of time that he's going to get stung. I can't get angry at the scorpion for being a scorpion, can I? Fuck yes, I can!

But I only have one way to address this anger, pull the lever on the escape hatch and say, "Fuck it, I'm outta here." I'm not going to do this, it's not sustainable, and it's not fair to ask this from someone who cares this much for you. I mean, who would say yes to that as a long-term arrangement anyway? I'm not doing it.

Faster, faster, faster on the bike, the anger flowing through my legs and arms, the bike becoming a missile as I fly down Flatbush toward the salt air and open sea.

How could she want this? I totally understand desiring someone who isn't your wife, girlfriend, husband, or boyfriend, but routinely acting on it in a one-on-one situation seems like the relationship equivalent of "hold my beer." She obviously doesn't cherish this relationship the way I do. She doesn't respect me! Doesn't she understand how rare it is to have a connection like this on so many levels? I want to shake some sense into her and tell her that I forbid it, but unfortunately (or probably fortunately), I don't have that authority. The toxic masculinity side of my personality is coming out strong.

The bike and I continue through the different neighborhoods, the demographics changing as I get further and further away from the center of the city, as the longer subway rides translate into lower rents. The street life here is palpable, nonstop movement and action to look at as I fly through the city, weaving in and out between cars, buses, and trucks. I'm one with the street and one with the bike.

Am I really going to walk away? Walk away from something that gives me so much joy and adventure? The thought of losing Jane sparks such a negative reaction in me that I feel like a man without options. My relationship with Jane is the most important thing to me—relationships above all else. When I think about doing almost anything, it's always better with Jane there.

I think about a recent weekend we had together, in a Bushwick warehouse dancing all night to deep house music while high on ecstasy the first night, at a friend's dinner party the other night. All the lovely mornings in bed, cooking breakfast, debating anything and everything. Oh, the coffee in bed!

I think about the trip we took together to Utah, driving around in my old pickup truck to various climbing spots, camping out in the open under the stars in the desert. We climbed highly technical routes like Ancient Art, Independence Monument, Sixshooter Peak, and Castleton Tower. Names that would mean nothing to you if you're not a climber, but they're the greatest hits of sandstone tower climbing in Utah. A trip like that was something I had never done with anyone I was sexually involved with before. We went mountain biking in Moab and it blew her mind when she saw Slickrock for the first time. I took her to the Grand Canyon and we fucked on the northern rim, standing up with both of us facing out into the deep abyss all around us.

I think about all the silly photos Jane and I took on our trips. She would always pop her head into the frame of the picture sideways. I have no idea why she liked to do that, but I loved it. She could be really goofy when she wanted to. Trips and adventures like that are not something I want to give up.

Not to mention, I've been living the best sex life I could possibly imagine.

Since our weekend retreat in upstate New York, it's just been getting better and better. I think about that weekend and how she said to me, "I'm not the kind of girl who has a boyfriend." But now I recall something else she said: "They always want to change me." When I heard those words at the time, they just floated away because I didn't think they applied to me. I was an evolved male, who would never try to make his girlfriend behave the way he felt was appropriate.

My head falls and I look down at the pavement passing underneath me. She knew exactly what was coming the whole time. Men have been doing this to her for her entire life and she has zero patience for it. Ugh, am I the same as all the others? Well, I haven't tried to change her, but I have to admit I have been expecting her to change of her own accord.

My pace continues to slow as I near the southern end of Brooklyn, where the traffic and street life start fading away. I'm leaving the business district of Flatbush Avenue behind me, and I'm into the wetlands and marshes of Jamaica Bay, which separates the Rockaways from Brooklyn. The six-lane thoroughfare becomes a two-lane road that works its way out the last couple of miles to the coast.

I ride past Floyd Bennett Field, the old WWII airstrip, with its aging hangars and abandoned military buildings, past the marinas and seafood restaurants. It's a different New York City out here. At the ass end of Brooklyn, I ride up the incline of the Marine Parkway Bridge, which will take me to the edge of the city, the edge of the state, and the wide-open ocean.

As I crest the bridge, the sound of seagulls, the breeze, and the smell of the ocean take me back to early childhood, when my family would spend every August at a house out on Fire Island, a barrier island further east along the Long Island shore.

Coasting down the backside of the bridge, I arrive at the Rockaways, where everything is covered in sand. The ride did its job. I've gotten my head to the calm place it needed to be, no cutting required.

Sand and Surf and All That Childhood Shit

From the bridge, it's an easy roll the last quarter mile to the beach, where I have my first unbroken view of the ocean and waves. A steady breeze blows from the west and the beachgoers have set up their umbrellas to combat sand blowing in from that direction. I lock the bike, take my shoes off, and walk out to the edge of the ocean and sit down. The parade of waves comes at me, one by one, and the sound of the breakers hitting the beach washes over me, enveloping me as if I was playing in them.

> *Excerpt from Jane's blog:*
> Very early on—and against the advice of many well-intentioned friends, relatives, teachers, and lovers—I decided that in the war between staying true to myself and making sure I fit in so others would like me, myself wins. Authenticity was more important than popularity. Popularity

without authenticity was worthless. I was sure that
if I was true to myself and loved myself, there
would be some people who would love me for
who I was.

I'm just like all the others—she changes or I walk. When I say it out loud, it doesn't sound right. But if her behavior is outside of how I want to live, then I should walk. But is it? Is her behavior outside of how I want to live? Or am I just an insecure man who can't handle his girlfriend sleeping with other men because of my jealousy? Because I'm afraid of what I think it says about me?

I know I've been doing my best to ignore the fact that Jane has been sleeping with other men, so perhaps my initial negative emotional reaction was too quick. I have to admit to myself that I haven't thought through whether an open-as-fuck relationship is even right for me. What would that actually look like? I visualize a future where I have lovers on the side. Lots of affirming sexual encounters with a variety of women that add to a rich life full of fantastic experiences: I can see that reality stretching into the future, and it feels kinda good.

But then I start visualizing Jane with her future lovers and a *lot* of jealousy comes up almost immediately. Interestingly, it occurs to me that knowing about her past sexual exploits has always turned me on. Even the story about the time with the twelve guys kinda got me excited when I didn't think *too* hard about it. There's something very erotic to me about a woman who's that turned on by raw sex. I also know those experiences have made her a sexual powerhouse and now I'm reaping the rewards. Shouldn't I feel the same way about her future exploits? What is my subconscious assuming about those future encounters? What negative outcome fantasy is my brain imagining will be the logical result? Am I fearful of losing intimacy with the woman I've been growing close to? Is it that I've finally found something really satisfying and I'm fearful of anything that could possibly disrupt it?

These questions swirl around in my head. I know I don't want to be in a completely monogamous relationship, so on some level an open or flexible relationship is an authentic lifestyle for me. What's the problem here? Is it just that she's too open for me? That her level of non-monogamy isn't the "correct amount"? Well, what is the correct amount? The correct amount, obviously, would be the amount that keeps me in my comfort zone, the amount that I could easily deal with. I laugh at myself when my logic brings me to that point and look out at the waves. A contentment washes over me in the way that it does after your own absurdity smacks you in the face. How could I still be such a moronic ape at the wizened age of 42?

So how much of this discomfort is tied up in my own insecurities? I've certainly battled impostor syndrome in my life, and our situation has all the ingredients to bring it to the surface. Jane is the "most popular girl" at the "high school" of my NYC nightlife, and just about every guy who meets her wants to hook up with her. That's intimidating to me because I know, as do they, that as long as she finds them attractive, Jane is in a lot of cases willing to do just that. At some level I've been reverting to my geeky-redheaded-child self, feeling like I'm not high enough on the org chart, and the more she hangs out with other guys, the more she'll recognize that. I shake my head slowly, Childhood shit still fucking me up.

There's another factor feeding my impostor syndrome: I am, for the first time in my adult life, the sexual neophyte in the relationship. I've had no real experience as an adult being the inexperienced one, and I've had no recent experience trying to level up my sexual activities to where my partner is, leveling it up to something that doesn't seem all that natural. But I also recognize that my ideas of what's natural or not are arbitrary and are probably based in a large part on my socialization as I was growing up. I'm going to have to let go of certain ideas I have about what the "right" way to live is.

And while I have always known about my insecurities—feeling like I was an impostor, trying to impress other people and gain validation from them—and have made real strides as an adult to address these issues, Jane coming into my life is making me fully aware of the hold they have on me. This connection with her is exposing some rot in my psyche, and I'm not liking what I'm seeing. This is not the person I thought I was.

I can also see that at this point in our sexual lives, I need more intimacy than Jane does, and she needs more novelty and adventure. When I was younger, I was probably closer to her level, seeking out adventure in my relationships more than security. Since Jane is twelve years younger than I am, I can understand her position, and I need to be sympathetic to where she is in her life.

I'm going to have to admit that my initial reaction—that Jane doesn't respect the relationship or me—is not valid. This is her coming at her life authentically, and her need for a completely open relationship is not a rejection of me, nor is it a rejection of the relationship. It's just who she is, and the scorpion was being kind in letting me know ahead of time that giving her a ride would definitely involve my getting stung a bit. (And yes, she happens to be a Scorpio—what are the chances.)

Another thing to consider is when I've tried to talk to Jane about my feelings of jealousy or insecurity, it hasn't gone very well. After I introduced Jane to climbing, she started training at the indoor climbing gym in her university town. One weekend, we were planning to spend the afternoon climbing there. But over breakfast that morning, she told me that the week before she had fucked the pro who ran the place.

"Really? I don't think I'm comfortable going to the gym this afternoon."

"Oh? Why is that?"

"It would be an awkward situation for me, to be at the gym with someone who is becoming my girlfriend and the guy who runs the place is fucking her when I'm not around. Why would I want to have all these emotions swirling around when I'm trying to have a fun workout with you?"

"Okay, I can see not wanting to have 'emotions swirling around' when you're trying to have fun, but why would it bring up so many emotions? It's just sex. I don't understand why it's such a big deal."

"It's the conflict that will be going on in my head. I've seen this guy a couple times now, and it's a bit of a pissing contest with him when I'm in the gym. Now in his eyes, he's got one up on me. The Neanderthal in my head will feel that and want to go physically confront him, but the intense conflict comes from knowing that's unacceptable, especially in this situation."

"Oh, you poor men with your fragile egos. Babe, don't you know sex is not a zero-sum game? Besides, I'm with you, not him. Nothing's been taken away from you, regardless of if he thinks so. This is only as big a deal as *you* make of it. Let's just go climb and get a fun workout in."

Her response left an impression on me. Was she right? Was I being too fragile? Am I weak emotionally? Should this be no big deal? I did want to punch him though.

As we got deeper into each other, I started realizing that if I wanted to keep this going, I needed to keep my emotional difficulties stemming from our open-as-fuck relationship to myself. She seems to have no capacity, or desire, to understand them. This is going to make the leap to the kind of relationship that Jane wants all the more treacherous for me. Am I really willing to get involved with someone whom I can't talk to about my own difficulties and challenges with the relationship, and how they are affecting the relationship for me?

What is Jane asking of me? And what are my own needs and limits? When I boil it all down it seems like those are the important questions to consider. What she needs in a relationship feels emasculating in a very real way. Jane has made it clear that her non-monogamy is public. Not hiding who she is, is an important part of who she is. Do I want to be working on this emotional challenge nearly every day of my life? To be constantly reminded that my girlfriend is hooking up with other men, to have no safe zone? How would this affect how I feel about who I am? How would this affect how I think about my own masculinity? How would this affect the quality of life I've come to appreciate in my world? How would I explain to friends and family that Jane can't make it tonight because she's fucking someone she picked up on the subway this afternoon?

This is so far beyond my experience that I'm not sure whether I can do it. It was one thing to click a button and come out of the closet about being in an open relationship; it's another thing to face the day-to-day realities of your girlfriend fucking other men *and* everybody you know possibly knowing about it.

It feels like a total surrender of my manhood, as if I'm sliding all the way over to the Sensitive New Age Guy side of the bland-to-toxic masculinity continuum. Of course, being the type of guy who tells his girlfriend what she can and cannot do to protect my ego would be like sliding all the way over to the Bro side, "just like all the other guys," as Jane put it. Neither proposition is attractive to me, so how can I find the strength that will allow me to exist as the Fierce Gentleman, classy and independent of my girlfriend's actions, the point on the continuum that I so desire to live at?

I have no idea.

I know that attempting an open-as-fuck relationship with Jane would put me in very uncomfortable terrain, which means that the journey itself would probably bring about significant personal growth in the very areas I need it most.

I stop.

Here it is, the thought I have been methodically working toward. This is the *key* thing for me. This *is* the attraction: Learning how to get past being the redheaded geek on the playground. Learning how to be independent of second-party validation. Learning how to get past the impostor syndrome. These are the issues that have been holding me back, and this terrifying journey is an opportunity to address them.

But at its heart, the journey is going through life with the woman I care about and want to be with. It will also probably be one hell of an adventure, in and out of the bedroom. When I put aside the anger, I can feel the attraction of the ask, the attraction of the fear, and it's obvious to me that I'm being drawn to these elements of the situation. Going forward feels challenging, exciting, and authentic.

Looking beyond the obvious challenges, can I envision a crazy life like this where I'm also maintaining a strong, loving, intimate relationship with the woman I want to be with? Is it possible that together we would be stronger, that I could rely on Jane to have my back as I continue to take risks on my own professional journey? Could this sort of non-monogamy deepen a relationship in a way I've never considered? Or would I lose my sense of self in order to be in this relationship? That wouldn't be sustainable for me or for the relationship.

Feeling the surf at my feet, I continue to consider all of these ideas, eventually coming back to a question that has always been a touchstone for me: What will I be missing out on if I let fear and the natural desire to stay in the comfort zone direct my decisions?

As I begin to embrace the challenge, my mind keeps pushing back against the idea that an open-as-fuck relationship is natural or possible or acceptable. I think back to conversations with my monogamous male friends, who kept telling me I was foolish to be engaging in non-monogamy with Jane. My friend Doug once said to me, "Look, I want to sleep with other women too, it's natural, but I'm mature enough to keep it under control."

I know he was trying to help, but it didn't really land the way he was hoping it would. In my most mature way, I responded that I valued adventure in my sex life, and I wouldn't be able to stay happy in a fully traditional relationship such as his, any more than I'd be able to stay happy if I gave up all my various travels and adventures. It wasn't a question of self-control, but how I wanted to live my life. This is who *I* am. Using that same logic, I should be able to see that Jane's level of non-monogamy has nothing to do with me—it's just an expression of who she is and what she needs to be happy living her life.

This was a critical insight. I couldn't authentically be with someone and ask them to be who they are not, just so I could feel secure. Especially, as I'm now reasoning, if those feelings of security are very possibly based on false narratives and issues that I haven't addressed in my own psyche. Oddly, it occurs to me that Doug's comment did help, just not in the way he intended.

Then there is the very real question of what my alternatives are. Go out and find another woman who I'm this well matched with, and whose engagement with non-monogamy happens to exactly match my own? That's not realistic, and it gets me thinking, Would I rather be the one being pulled forward or the one doing the pulling? Since my early twenties, I've always been the one doing the pulling, always the one being shamed and feeling like the freak, so now I have the opportunity to see it from the other side, and, I hope, respond in a different fashion. I'm sure there is a girlfriend or two in my history saying I'm finally getting a taste of my own medicine.

Could I start thinking of Jane's casual-sex exploits as life-affirming experiences rather than as threats to mine? I think of how affirming some of my own experiences have been. When I began engaging in casual sex for the right reasons, for authentic reasons, it improved my life satisfaction, which improved my relationships with friends, family, and lovers. That's a real thing. Similarly, climbing for the right reasons brought me more satisfaction than climbing for the wrong reasons. I need intense experiences—whether it's extreme sports, traffic dodging on my bike, or sex—to live a happy life.

If that's true for me, I should be able to see that for Jane too.

All this thinking is starting to move Jane's open-as-fuck relationship model from the scary impossible to the scary possible. Possible because I'm starting to understand her motivations.

Possible because I know I like to be challenged. Scary because, holy fuck, this means I'm voluntarily going to have dig deep to tie my sense of self, and my sense of what it means to be a man, to different measures. In my life I've learned that anything worth doing takes effort and some amount of suffering, and there is no reason this should be any different.

I stand up and start walking down the beach, the breakers on one side of me, the children playing in the sand on the other, and my mind settles on the sound of the waves, crashing on the beach, over and over again.

Brain, Body, and Heart. The trifecta of any attraction. At different points in my life, I've needed each one in varying amounts. Although to be honest, the body seems to have always been in the forefront of my decision making. My carnal desires have driven a lot of my relationship decisions, as well as some life ones. And definitely not always for the better.

At first, I was pursuing Jane for needs of the body. Sure, she was intelligent and had a lot to offer but it was her raw sexuality that first drew me in. It's true, at some level I did think of her as a magical sex fairy. As we got closer, I began to get the needs of the brain met as well. But the more I got to know Jane, the more obvious it became that while she was certainly capable of returning needs of the heart in her own Eastern European way, she had no understanding of what her lifestyle was going to put me through emotionally, and didn't seem to care, at least not very much. "Oh, you poor men with your fragile egos." Those words are still rattling around in my head.

A driving force in my life has been a palpable fear of missing out. That fear is hyperamplified when it comes to sex. I want to experience all that sex has to offer and I've been searching for those experiences. Then Jane came along and presented me all of the possibilities in a single package, with just a couple of scary issues included at no extra cost: the difficulties and emotional challenges her sleeping with other men would cause me, and her lack of empathy for those difficulties. This means I'm going to have to figure things out on my own.

And this is the Faustian bargain I've been presented with. Given what I've been through in my life I'm convinced that I can get by without her support on these issues, and that eventually her intelligence will carry her through to the point of emotionally understanding them. With enough time and experience, she'll evolve into the empathetic, mature, emotionally developed state that I'm obviously at. It simply needs to be unlocked by life with a loving partner, me, in a strong relationship, even one as strange as ours is shaping up to be.

As for the risks, I can see now, all these years later, that I assessed them that day on the beach with a certain amount of arrogance. I'd taken so many physical risks over the years that emotional risks seemed insubstantial in comparison. I'd faced death, and feelings couldn't kill me, right? That "damn the torpedoes, full speed ahead" attitude toward emotional pain made it a lot easier for me to make the decision. It might be painful, but that pain was far enough in the future, and somewhat theoretical.

If I hadn't been so taken with her, I might have paid more attention to what she was really asking of me. At some level she was asking me to grow up, which was a good thing. But it was obvious she was also telling me that she wouldn't have any patience for the complicated emotions I knew I would be facing in this relationship. She just didn't want to hear it. I know now that I was glossing over just how difficult that would be for me, and I wasn't able to recognize the sort of barrier that would place between us.

I turn around and start walking back to my spot on the beach. My thinking has brought me to a place where I'm going forward, knowing full well this could be psychologically and emotionally intense. But the deliberate decision feels like it accurately represents who I am and how I want to live my life.

I get back to my bike, unlock it, and start my ride across the bridge and back home, but at a much more relaxed pace. Jane is going to move in soon and her lifestyle isn't going to change. I let that sink in. I try to convince myself that I'm making a rational decision with lots of thought process behind it, but in actuality, part of me realizes that I was always going to say yes. It's just too much of an adventure to turn down. I'll figure it out; I know I will. Well, I'm fairly sure I will anyway.

As I ride back on Bedford Avenue, I pass the old right field wall of Ebbets Field, home of the Brooklyn Dodgers. When they tore the ballpark down after the Dodgers went to California, they left the right field wall up and integrated it into the housing complex they built on the site. As a kid, my dad had spent many an afternoon watching the Dodgers in that stadium. I can read the sign as it stands now, "Ebbets Field Apartments," a far cry from the glory of the World Series champions of 1955. I keep on riding.

Bikes unlocked freedom for me in New York City as a kid. I fell in love with riding and at 16 got a job at a bike shop. My friends and I lived and breathed biking in the city back then. I bought this bike when I was 17. It's taken plenty of scrapes and dings in countless falls and collisions and general abuse over the years. Yet here it is, still going strong. I've kept it alive time and time again, always fixing it, always modifying it, always loving it. I feel at home when I ride it through the city. I feel like we both belong here, together. Could I imagine my life here without it? Could I imagine my life without the freedom and adventure that this bicycle has given me? I cycle uphill to the crest of Eastern Parkway and then coast downhill on Bedford, watching the world go by, enjoying the spectacle, on my way home.

Act I, Scene 325

It's night. Adam and Jane are in Jane's bedroom in the house she shares at her university. They are lying in bed. The distant voices of her roommates are audible from the kitchen.

JANE: So school is ending soon. Do I go back home, or do you want to move in together?

ADAM: I want to move in together.

JANE: Are you going to be able to deal with my sex life when we're on top of each other like that?

ADAM: I don't know. To be sure, it's a lot, and honestly, I didn't realize it would continue at this level.

JANE: I like what we have but I'm not interested in changing, nor could I.

ADAM: I'm seeing that, and intelligently wouldn't want you to change who you are. I'd like to believe I'd leave before I'd ask that.

JANE: So again, I pose the question, how are you going to deal with my sex life?

ADAM: Well, you know I'm out west working a lot. Once we move in, could you confine your extracurriculars to when I'm out of town?

(*Jane considers the proposal.*)

JANE: Yeah, I could do that for a while, I think. Seems like a reasonable compromise for now. Is that it?

ADAM: Actually, no, that's not it. My close friends are off-limits.

JANE: Why?

ADAM: Because those relationships are too important to me to risk them. One of the things you've said that you love about me is my ability to create and maintain deep friendships. Well, this is one of those ways—understanding their value and that it's foolish to put them at risk just so you can get laid with every person you want to.

JANE: Okay, no close friends, but you can fuck any of my friends, just so you know.

ADAM: Good talk.

ACT II

Chapter 4
Ignorance Is Bliss

Oh, that smell, that glorious smell. I'm lying in bed with my eyes closed. Jane is holding a mug under my nose, and I sink into that place of perfect bliss. Being woken up by a fresh cup of coffee is absolutely one of my greatest pleasures in life. My eyes open to see her sitting on the bed in her T-shirt, smiling at me, always happy when she manages to get the coffee ready without waking me up. It's one of the rare occasions that she does the honors, as I am almost always up before her. I accept the cup as an offering to our black coffee connection.

She pulls back the velvet curtains she had made, to softly illuminate the room with the early morning light. As she slides them to either side, I hear the telltale sound of the metal grommets scraping along the black metal plumbing pipe I had hung to support the heavy curtains. I look up at the high ceilings of our bedroom and I'm reminded of the acrobatics I went through to hang the pipe. It took some effort, but in all fairness to her, she was right. The thick red curtains added the softness and coziness the cavernous room needed.

Jane climbs back into bed with me. Our legs mingle under the soft sheets, and I grasp her hand in mine. Taking a sip of the hot coffee, I am fully immersed in my world of sensation, emotion, and peace as we sit there in silence, enjoying our morning time together. I know how this scene will end, but the anticipation keeps the entire process at a slightly higher vibration for me.

Two years in and I still cannot get enough of this woman physically, but it's these moments—when all the wildness has fallen away, where time slows down into the foreplay of love and intimacy, and we're left with just the basics of living together—which give deeper meaning to what will shortly follow, the sweaty engagement of our bodies between these sheets that she got on sale.

But last night was a different story. In bed getting ready to watch a movie, Jane got a text. As she read and responded to it, I could tell from her body language that it was a new, or potentially new, lover. For a few minutes she went back and forth before turning to me and happily launching into the story of her hookup with him. She was on the subway platform waiting for the train when she had eye contact with him and started up a conversation. She continued and I tried to show that I was listening while doing my best to transform the words into a foreign language so as not to comprehend their meaning.

Jane finished, and I said something meaningless like "Fun!" and then abruptly went into the kitchen to make some tea for the movie. I don't drink tea. Whenever she did this, I wasn't sure what to do next, but generally I needed to walk away to gather my thoughts. Intellectually, I knew this is what I had signed up for, but I was always taken by surprise when it came up. I tried to let it go, but it always continued to nag me. It took a few minutes before the movie successfully distracted me.

That was stressful, but here I am now, enveloped in the deliciousness of our bedding and her limbs, which has the effect of making my response last night seem almost silly. How can both of these realities exist at the same time? How can I get to a point where hearing about these things doesn't cause such a visceral reaction in me?

Eventually, I move to the kitchen to make more espresso. As the machine heats up, I am captivated by the steam slowly rising up the face of the black kitchen cabinets.

Those first few months of living together were, for the most part, amazing. My tech company had closed a funding round and we were off to the races so I was in and out of town with work, and the weeks we spent together in the city were full of fun with each other and friends, lots of wild sex, and our home time together.

Yes, Jane was with other guys, but I was away when it happened, and tried my best not to think about it. When I was in town though, her phone was the hookup connection, and the notifications began to take on an ominous quality for me, provoking a Pavlovian response of low-grade fear, anger, and jealousy. That's when my brain would go through the complex gymnastics of distraction. Pay no attention to what's going on over there, nothing to see here. She was adhering to the compromise of not having sex with other people when I home, but the back-and-forth, both before and after these rendezvous, was always going on around me.

When she would share a story of a hookup with me, it was always a challenge to get through it. I would feign listening while trying not to hear it, and then, if possible, I would walk away to get my head back to a grounded state. It's funny now to see how much I was trying to avoid during this period, but perhaps I knew that I needed to initially. It was a way to get through until Jane stopped needing that amount of casual sex or I figured out how to get to a point where it didn't bother me anymore.

I Do Until I Don't

When Jane moved in, we had five months till her student visa ran out. Our plan was that we'd live together for that time and if we hadn't killed each other by then, we would get married.

> Act II, Scene 38
> *It's morning. Adam is working at the desk, staring at lines of computer code. Jane comes in.*
>
> **JANE:** Well, it's time to make the decision. Do you want to keep me here?
>
> **ADAM,** *not looking up from the computer*: Yep.
>
> **JANE:** So we'll get married?

ADAM, *turning to look at Jane*: Yes.

JANE: Cool. How about Thursday?

ADAM: Works for me.

On Wednesday evening I went over to my parents' house to let them know that we were getting married the next day. They immediately wanted to throw us a party, which we were adamantly against. I told them if we made it ten years, they could throw us one then. I felt bad disappointing them, but a wedding reception wasn't really our thing. The best I could do for them was say they could come to the ceremony and take us out to a late lunch afterward.

On Thursday morning Jane left early to have some time to herself, and I stayed at the house working. I took the subway downtown and met her at the Marriage Bureau of the City Clerk's Office. Neither of us had given much weight to the idea of "legal" marriage, which made for kind of an ironic situation. If we wanted to stay together, which we did, we were going to have to cross that boundary, so there we were, in all the ridiculousness that we both felt, which caused us to burst out laughing the moment we saw each other.

Jane showed me a new silver ring that she had purchased that morning to commemorate the event. It was always wonderful when I got to see her emotionally intimate side. It warmed my heart to find out she did not view this as just a bureaucratic necessity.

Take a number. That's what the sign said when we walked into the big room just off the main entry into the massive municipal building. We took one, and then sat down in the waiting room with all the other couples. Lots of men in tuxedos and women in ornate white wedding dresses. We definitely stood out as different. Jane wore a flowy, long, bright red shirt over tights and black boots. I thought it was coincidental that she wore red, but she had specifically chosen it. Oddly, I was the one in white. It was my favorite shirt, given to me by a previous lover, which Jane thought was rather apropos.

The idea of marriage held little weight for me, but there was still something very real about the decision. Even if it ended up being short-term, it was a reconsecration of my determination to make this connection work. Our connection was brilliant on so many levels and yet there was always this darkness lurking off to the side.

But I also had to acknowledge that she was willing to compromise with me on important things. All the signs indicated that she was committed to trying to make this work, so I had to recognize that and made a conscious decision to continue to push myself. Yet I could see how I was trying to keep my head in the sand as much as possible, which really wasn't in the spirit of why I got into this. Jane was Jane and I was me. We needed to meet in the middle, or at least close-ish to it, not make sure that Adam avoids anything painful.

This was also the first time I had ever been in a relationship with someone who didn't think of me as a freak for my sexuality, or my outside adventures, and accepted me for who I was. Here was a woman who got excited for me when I said I wanted to take off for a few weeks on a surfing or mountain adventure, who didn't see my desire to live my own life as a rejection of her, but as something unique and positive about me. And I felt all these ways about her—except for the sex she was having without me. I needed to learn how to see it the same way I saw (and for that matter, the same way she saw) my adventures, and not take it as a statement about our connection or even me.

As I continued to wait for our turn, I wondered, Was this seeking the risk in its purest form? Or was this just taking hits for misguided reasons? I knew growth was going to be painful. And I felt that this pain had the potential to produce the kind of changes in me I wanted. These experiences, if I could successfully navigate them, could transform me into the man I wanted to be.

It seemed the only way to get there, though, was through a trial by fire. Jane wasn't going to provide a lot of emotional support for what I was navigating, but luckily for me, Sylvie, who had been my girlfriend when I had first met Jane, and who had since become one of my best friends, was there as my sounding board. She had been helping me navigate some of my earlier difficulties with Jane, although she didn't have any personal experience with what I was dealing with. In fact nobody I knew did. But she was sympathetic and nonjudgmental, and she cared a lot about me. Here was the safe connection I needed to disclose my feelings. Sylvie became my confidant, and I credit her with keeping me at it several times when I wanted to quit.

The cynic in me wonders if Sylvie was enjoying my getting a taste of my own medicine. Maybe she was a little (and I wouldn't fault her for that) but Sylvie was a caring individual and her concern was genuine. She saw how well-matched Jane and I were in so many ways, and she recognized the ways I hoped the relationship would help me grow. She really leaned hard on me not to give up, and I didn't give up. So here we were at the Marriage Bureau, Jane, Sylvie, who was acting as our witness, my parents, and me.

The room was quite an international affair, a cross section of all the different worlds and cultures that make up the melting pot of New York City. There were more languages being spoken around us than we could count. No matter what walk of life everyone was from, we were all there for the same purpose, and there was a piece of me that felt good to be part of it.

"I do, until I don't" is what Jane and I had agreed on. We both felt that it seemed to be the most rational way to look at it. Soon our number was called, and the adventure began.

The first room we entered was unceremoniously bland. A clerk asked us some questions and gave the three of us some paperwork to sign. From there we were ushered into another waiting room, where we presented our signed paperwork and sat down. It was all very bureaucratic and matter-of-fact. There was nothing to suggest that what was taking place in these halls were attempts at lifelong commitment.

Our names got called and we went into the "chapel" for the ceremony. The officiant was standing behind a podium. When we approached, she asked us if we had rings to give each other. We did not. She gave a brief synopsis of the event and said that she was going to ask us to declare our intent to marry each other. Then came the famous lines, "Do you take this . . . blah blah blah . . . to be your . . . blah blah blah. . . . I now pronounce you husband and wife."

Wow. Husband and wife.

Those words landed. I kissed her. Done. The entire thing lasted less than a minute and that was it, we were married.

As we were walking out of the ceremony, Jane said under her breath to me, "Do you think we'll make it a year?" I laughed and saw in her candor just why I was with this woman. And although getting married was fun and silly at some level, it still felt like I had just burned my boats behind me. No going back now, or not easily anyway.

Back out in the hallway, there was an area to take pictures with scenes of NYC on the wall behind you, which we did to make sure we were getting the full experience. Jane threw the bouquet that my mom had brought her, and Sylvie caught it. My parents were beaming, as they never thought that they would see this day. Many years ago, I had told my dad I was never getting married, which he made sure to remind me of over and over again.

The five of us walked west to Church Street in TriBeCa and had lunch in one of our favorite restaurants at the time. In the end, no matter how hard we tried to avoid it, we did end up at Church on our wedding day.

After lunch we said goodbye to my parents. Then Sylvie got a cab to take the three of us to a small oyster bar we liked in the West Village. There Jane's best friend, also a previous lover, joined us and brought along fresh cupcakes from a top artisanal bakery in the area. Sylvie bought us a couple of bottles of champagne, and while we were making toasts, the bar brought out a tray of oysters for us on the house.

The couple who had first brought Jane over to our apartment when Sylvie and I were living together came by to say hi. It was a lovely way to spend the evening. Later that night, lying in bed together, after making sure we had consummated the marriage, we marveled that the entire day—including lunch, cabs, champagne, cupcakes, and subway rides—had cost less than $600.

At a party a few days later, Jane introduced me as her husband, which sounded strange but also, I had to admit to myself, kinda fun. Then, when I put her on my health insurance, I was surprised at how comforting it was. Somehow we had leveled up our connection without meaning to and both seemed to like it. I could see that we were starting to lean into the idea of being married. The joke that we thought we considered marriage to be was apparently on us.

***

Halloween in NYC, one of the best nights of the year if you like to be out and about and know where to go, or more important, where *not* to go. Luckily, Jane always knew the best underground warehouse spot to go to. We invited a group of our friends from out west to come in for the weekend, a group of about eight in all. Jane and I rented an apartment in our building from a neighbor, and we all stayed together for the weekend with blow-up mattresses spread out on the floor of both apartments.

They flew in on Thursday, and we spent the next two days running around the city, seeing art and theater and staying up way too late doing bumps of cocaine. In the background, the news was alive with updates on a massive storm that was bearing down on us. We assumed it would be as anticlimactic as predictions of weather Armageddon usually were, but it turned out that Superstorm Sandy had New York City in its sights.

The big party was on Saturday night, in a massive warehouse right on the East River. We showed up around 10:30 p.m. just as the rain from Sandy was beginning to fall. The dance area had a wall of speakers mounted on the side of a bus if you can believe it, pumping out crystal-clear deep house music that made your soul groove. And yeah, about this time, the ecstasy was kicking in. Jane and I danced together all night to amazing music, high on drugs and having a blast with our friends.

By the time we left the party, it was 8 a.m. We walked outside to find the rain and wind hammering down on us. There were cops everywhere, telling people to go home and get off the streets. We all headed back to the apartments to eat and get some sleep, still thinking our guests were going to make their flight out later that day. But as we were making brunch back in our apartment, the wind kept on picking up, knocking limbs down from trees.

That's around the time we heard that the airports were closing down and all flights were canceled. Nobody was getting out of the city that day.

By evening, a state of emergency had been declared, but you wouldn't have been able to tell from the mood in our apartment with all our friends. Still feeling the drugs and high on a fabulous weekend, we spread out blankets in our living room. One of our friends made a screen by taping sheets of printer paper together and Jane grabbed an old academic projector she had so we could watch movies together. We ate leftovers and made loads of popcorn. It was a great time.

Monday came and the storm made landfall, wreaking havoc all over the city. The East River had flooded its banks, leaving large swaths of the Lower East Side underwater. A massive short at a power station on East 14th Street lit up the stormy night, sending huge sparks high into the sky. Power went out over much of the city that night. At our home everyone was still there, and we were making the most of it. But after two days of us all trapped, and our fifth day together, with the drugs having worn off, tensions were starting to flare a bit.

Jane had a big blowup with the girlfriend of one of our friends, and by Tuesday evening we were all a bit frayed. To make matters worse, Jane had to cancel a date she had been looking forward to, which added to her frustration, which she was vocal about.

I was simmering with my own frustrations, too. Normally, I'd combat my emotional reactions to Jane's needs by throwing myself into a solo adventure in the backcountry. But I was stuck in the city. We were both trapped and annoyed, with a lot of people in our space, and unable to get what we wanted and needed.

After three days of this, the walls were starting to feel like they were closing in. But the storm had finally broken, and the sun was out. I suggested that she and I take the bikes and ride around Lower Manhattan to see the damage. Once we started riding in the brilliant sun, it was almost immediately apparent that this was the right move. Our lightness returned and we were two kids having fun together on our bikes. The "emergency vehicles only" order was still in effect, so there was no car traffic, and we moved around easily, standing on our bikes, riding with no hands, arms stretched above us and going straight down the center of the streets and avenues.

It was eerie being out and about in an NYC with no power and no cars. The traffic lights were dark and all the signs off; there was no loud music playing, no car horns. The only normal city noise was the occasional siren.

We were riding uptown on Hudson Street when we noticed that Rivoli Pizzeria, at the corner of Christopher Street, had its doors open and there seemed to be a lot of people inside. We locked the bikes and went in. Sure enough, they were open and making pizza. They had candles lit everywhere, and their gas-fired ovens were working. They needed to use up the ingredients in the refrigerators before they went bad so they were selling slices with any toppings you wanted for $1.

It was a party-type atmosphere in there. Everyone was talking, laughing, sharing stories about the storm, a sense of community I had rarely seen in New York City. We ordered a couple of slices and sat down at a small table. Following true NYC pizza etiquette, I folded the slice in half and took a bite. My mouth went into orgasm. The crust was perfect, the sauce so flavorful. There was just the right amount of cheese and the pepperoni was exactly the right amount of spicy. We looked into each other's eyes and just started laughing. Whatever unscratched itches we had been feeling were instantly scratched. It was the most perfect moment, with the perfect person, and it was accompanied by the most perfect slices of pizza we had ever had.

The Worst Sound I Ever Heard

Jane is speaking to the doctor while they are reviewing the X-rays. I can't understand a word they're saying because they're speaking Spanish, and rapidly. They keep looking at me and then at the X-rays of my neck. All around me is the mayhem of a rural hospital in Central America, the only one within three hours in any direction.

I'm a little bleary eyed and in pain, but Jane has it all under control. I'm just so happy that she managed to get me off the beach, into the car, and drive the ninety minutes to get here on unfamiliar back roads in an unfamiliar country. I was happy to be a passenger. Hell, I was happy just to be able to move my legs.

Three hours ago, we were having the time of our lives, surfing off the remote end of the Azuero Peninsula in Panama.

It was day seven of our trip and we had been spending the morning surfing easy breakers in the protected cove near our camp spot in the jungle. Jane was starting to get hang of it and could pretty much stand up on any wave she caught. I was looking forward to many more surf trips together.

Jane caught a really nice wave and had a huge smile on her face as she was flying along. I caught the crappy wave following hers just so I could meet her by the beach. As I flew past her, she sprayed me with water and laughed. I was kind of looking back at her and not paying attention to the wave when it broke a little unexpectedly and threw me headfirst off the board.

Barely an instant after hitting the water, I heard the sound of my own neck breaking as the entire weight of my body came down on my head. The full realization of what had just happened began to sink in even before my body had a chance to collapse into the shallow water. Face down, limp, and shocked, I could hear Jane laughing, not realizing what had happened.

Flooded with pain, and with a level of trepidation that cannot possibly be described, I attempted to wiggle my fingers and toes. I felt a burst of joy when they responded to my command and wiggled. All was not lost yet, but I was helpless.

In a matter of moments, Jane figured out something was wrong. Moving quickly through the water, she reached me and got me far enough onto the beach so I wouldn't drown while we considered the situation. What struck me later on, as I lay in the hospital bed and had time to reflect, was Jane's lack of panic or intimidation.

She was on her knees, by my side, her hands lying gently on my arm. In what must have been a shaky, shocked voice, I said, "I think I broke my neck." She was focused and methodical. There was no cell service. The nearest town with a hospital was an hour and a half away, and I was in so much pain I could barely move, but we knew we had to get to the hospital.

I outweighed Jane by forty pounds, but she took all my weight and smoothly helped me up the steep embankment to get us off the beach and to the car. As I was trying to get comfortable in the passenger seat next to her, she turned the ignition, and I was so thankful she knew how to drive a stick shift. As she drove through the jungle on the remote dirt road, she was coolheaded enough to joke around, which completely relaxed me.

"Don't think you're getting out of fucking me just cause you have a broken neck. A girl has needs, you know."

For the rest of the drive, we settled into our normal banter, not letting the gravity of the situation affect us. The woman just didn't do panic.

On entering the mayhem of the emergency room, Jane continued her cool demeanor, keeping everything flowing with her fluent Spanish. Now here we were, looking at X-rays of my broken neck, Jane in charge, talking to the doctor, translating the highlights of the conversation for me. Like I said, I was happy to let her drive.

And there it was, that strength and confidence that was always there. You couldn't miss it. It had fascinated me and had drawn me in as I was getting to know her. Lying in that bed in the ER, I had some time to appreciate just how unshakable she was. Of course, that same strength, and the associated arrogance, on top of her determination to live her life unapologetically, caused me plenty of emotional pain too.

But living her life unapologetically meant she didn't ask anyone else to apologize for their life—as long as it was lived ethically. That strength meant I was never walking on eggshells around her, which was something new to me in a relationship. I'd never been close to anyone before who I felt I could be that relaxed with, who accepted me that completely. This was not someone who was constantly looking for some sign that I was going to betray them. I was overcome with love for her at that moment, completely forgetting about the dire situation I was in.

Luckily for me it was a clean break of the C7 vertebra, with nothing shifting at all from the impact. There was a fair amount of pain along the way, but over the next twelve weeks, the bone knit perfectly.

***

Yeah, I got really lucky with my neck, but I also knew I had to address the issue and take care of myself so that it could heal. Physical pain was something I understood far better than emotional pain. Over time the physical pain went away, as I took the necessary steps to make that happen. Basically the complete opposite of how I was addressing the emotional pain that was slowly creeping in.

I was starting to live an emotional dichotomy. At the same time that I was feeling like my life was a rocket ship headed straight up for the heavens, there was also a part of what was going on in my life that I was pretending wasn't happening. I was simply trying to ignore it. The signs kept appearing, and I kept trying to avert my eyes. Just stay in the happy place, Adam, and all will be okay. Ignorance is bliss, right?

Chapter 5
Adam in Wonderland

Excerpt from Adam's journal:

After ten days in the backcountry at base camp, high up in the mountains, a climbing buddy and I awoke to a beautiful morning with no clouds. We began hiking to the climb at 5 a.m., and by eight we were moving up it at a good tempo. Although quite challenging, the climb was going well, with some vertical ice pillars, decent rock, and easy snow sections. We were really having a blast with it. Some high clouds were starting to develop but we ignored them. Confident in our climbing ability and our speed, we figured we'd be off it before anything serious came in.

Within a few hours though, our clear gorgeous day had transformed into dark storm clouds. Maybe it was hubris, or boys being dumb boys, but we ignored the signs and thought it was better to finish the climb and walk off.

Much quicker than we were prepared for, a blizzard arrived, so intense that we could barely see. Far enough up the face at that point, we now had no choice but to finish the climb, rather than rappel the eight rope lengths down the mountain face in high winds and whiteout conditions.

An hour or so later we reached the top in weather like I had never seen while climbing. Unable to see the route to get down, shivering, and in waist deep snow with no snowshoes, we speculated that the easiest way off was down a steep gully that descended through some of the cliff bands we had seen on the hike in. Whether it was even passable in these conditions was unclear, but given the intensity of the situation, we figured that it was our best chance of survival.

Struggling through the snow, the only way to move is to swim through it, trying our best to stay on top. I am already tired from the seven and a half hours of moving and I am fighting for my life, desperately trying to see something that would indicate I'm going in the correct direction. It's taking ten minutes to go fifty meters and I am rapidly running out of energy to move as I finally make out the notch that I believe is the top of the descent gully. Entering what I hope is the way down, we begin stepping down the steep slope backward, still roped together so as not to lose one another in the whiteout.

Communication is impossible as we are separated by fifty feet of line in the swirling snow and abusive wind. Time has lost meaning. I am operating on autopilot, just putting one foot after the other: step down, step down, step down. I have no idea how long we've been descending the gully when a freight train of snow slams into me in the form of an avalanche. Tossed like a rag doll, I'm wiped off the face of the mountain and into the swirling void . . .

Sex parties were something that Jane enjoyed, and after Jane moved in, we started attending them together. It was one of the ways Jane (and I) could have casual sex with other people when we were both in NYC.

These were often big, lavish parties with hundreds of people. There just happened to be sex going on here and there—and more and more of it as the evening wore on. Jane quickly became a connoisseur of the city's sex party scene and was quite selective about which parties to go to. She favored ones that brought together a lively cross section of the sex-positive community. There were professionals, artists, performers, Wall Street types, burners, yuppies, hipsters, suburban couples who had moved out of the city to raise kids, and young singles who had come to the city to get away from the more conservative sections of the country. There was a remarkable range of ages, sexual orientations, and kink preferences. Basically, anyone who was a little adventurous about sex and was turned on by being open about it in that scene.-

Something about the environment at the parties we attended encouraged people to check at the door all the competition and hierarchy that defines so much of what goes on in NYC. The guy being tied up and whipped might be the CEO of some hedge fund during the day. The woman getting gangbanged on the bed might be teaching special needs kids on Monday morning. The ripped young guy who was commanding the living room scene might be a shipping clerk at a warehouse out in Queens. Only by talking with someone did you gain any sense of their place in the regular world, if they felt like telling you. The fantasies that they lived out at these parties probably helped ground them in their everyday lives. There was, I thought, a real human beauty in it.

At a good, well-run party, there was no pressure to physically engage at all, you could just move through the various rooms and observe as long as you were quiet and respectful to those playing. Many of the partygoers had an exhibitionist streak and got off on being watched as they engaged in their activities, I mean after all, people don't generally go to a sex party because they're looking for privacy. Being a voyeur was part of the symbiosis of the entire thing.

As much as I came to appreciate these parties, attending them with Jane was a challenge at first. Shortly after Jane moved in, she informed me that it was time to go to sex party together. She went on about how great it was going to be to have so many willing participants all in one place for us. Her enthusiasm was palpable, and it scared me a bit. We'd had other guys join us or swapped with a couple, but at a party like this, it seemed like I'd be seeing Jane's unconstrained sexual expression with another man, or men, when I wasn't part of it. I wasn't sure how I'd react, or whether I could handle it at all. What if my reaction would be so intense I'd have to bolt from the party, and maybe walk away from Jane altogether? That was a scary thought, but if I couldn't face up to Jane's desires, the relationship didn't have much of a future anyway. I had to assume there was some chance of this, but a deal is a deal, and this is what I had agreed to.

I mean, it's not like I wasn't excited by the idea of being able to have casual, objectified sex with a variety of available women, if that truly was what was going to take place. But then another fear began to emerge. What if everyone still had me pegged as that redheaded geeky kid on the playground? What if no one wanted to engage with me? I really had no idea what to expect.

The only other time I had been to anything like a sex party was several years earlier with a previous girlfriend. It had been an intimate affair in one largish room where everyone was sort of together. It ended up being a low-stress situation, as everyone knew we were complete novices, and they paid the two of us quite a bit of attention. I ignorantly assumed that what Jane and I would be going to would be a similar type of event, so when Jane said that she wanted us to be free to engage with whomever we wanted, I agreed, unaware of what I was getting myself into. For some reason I thought that we'd all be at least within line of sight of each other.

The night of that first party, getting ready in our apartment, there was a nervous energy to my antics, and I was trying my best to feign chillness. I had decided to wear black slacks with a white shirt and dark purple vest. Jane was in a sultry long gray dress with a slit along the side to show off a long, stunning leg and high-heel shoes.

The taxi dropped us off at the downtown hotel where the party was being held, and after being checked in at the door, we were escorted to a private elevator with two other couples, both quite sexy. After a thorough talk about consent and party etiquette, the hostess took us up to the penthouse suite. As the elevator inched its way upward, the numbers slowly counting to 18, the six of us stood there in slightly uncomfortable silence.

When the elevator doors opened, the first thing I saw, straight in front of me, was a gorgeous view of the NYC nighttime skyline through thirty-foot floor-to-ceiling windows. Cool, sexy deep music flooded the space at a volume that enveloped you but still allowed for easy conversation. It became quickly apparent that this was one of the classiest parties I had ever been to. Imagine an *Eyes Wide Shut* scenario but without all the misogyny and wealth discrimination.

As we walked around the party, taking it all in, we realized it was huge. The space consisted of three adjoining penthouse suites, the entire top floor of the hotel. There were all kinds of nooks, crannies, bedrooms, and small hallways, giving the party a slightly mysterious and catacomb-like atmosphere—but offset by different views of the city. Wherever we wandered, there were sexy women and men in lingerie serving hors d'oeuvres and champagne. Classy as fuck.

The almost three hundred attendees came in a variety of shapes, sizes, and ages, but everyone seemed to have a positive attitude about themselves and their bodies. This came through in the way folks dressed and presented themselves. The result was everyone was sexy in their own way, and the variety and sheer number of guests ensured that everyone could at least find someone they were aroused by.

We got drinks and began to mingle with the other partygoers. It definitely didn't hurt to have Jane as my date there, as she tended to draw people in with her looks and outgoing personality. As I warmed up to the environment and started getting comfortable in my skin, my conversations with the women we were talking to took on a far more flirtatious vibe. I was having a lot of fun conversing with a woman I was attracted to when Jane and the woman's husband said they were going to go off on their own. I decided not to think about the two of them and just focus on the woman I was with. Her eyes were holding mine with electric intensity. We chatted for a while before the conversation reached that awkward point where you are both ready to move on but are unsure how to exit gracefully.

The party kept rolling. I was chatting with these people here and that person there, and eventually hooked up with a woman, giving her an orgasm with my hand up her skirt from behind while pressing her body against one of the huge windows in the main room, sending her climax out over the city lights.

Jane and I kept coming back to each other to check in, doing our patented drop-and-deploy party experience, till at some point later in the evening, I realized it had been a bit of time since I had seen her. I went strolling around the party to find her, to do our check-in. I was really enjoying myself.

I passed through dance/DJ areas and through all of the party's various rooms. Sometimes I would pause at a particular spot and watch the events unfolding. In one room I saw a man tied up and whipped by a woman in a dominatrix outfit. In another bedroom, a woman was lying on her back with her legs spread and two men were taking turns going down on her. I realized that this was a competition between her husband and another man. They each had a minute before switching out. Back and forth they went, and the wife seemed to be in ecstasy. It was unclear to me if the couple knew the other man beyond the current interaction.

Eventually, I came upon a room and saw a woman naked on a bed with three men on her and a few people standing around and watching. As I approached the scene, I realized it was Jane, and I went numb. I averted my eyes and just kept walking, trying to pretend I hadn't seen what I saw.

Shocked and in a slight trance, I continued into an adjacent space, walked up to a window, and just stared out at the skyline. What the fuck was I doing? I was so shaken by the sight of Jane with the three men that I questioned if I was in the right place, or with the right woman. Also, I was now trapped. There was no way back to the main area of the party without going through the scene that Jane was having. I took a sip of my drink trying to figure out where I was on this journey.

I had no idea how to process the event and somehow even managed to rationalize the fact that the woman I had given that orgasm to had shortly thereafter sucked my cock in the coat closet. I could feel my self-righteousness kicking in. I had hooked up at an appropriate level, but three guys at once? That was too much. By the time I finished that last thought, though, my hypocrisy hit me over the head. It reminded me of something Jane had said: "If you want to be with me, then you really need to be with all of me. And if you're having emotional reactions to my lifestyle, well then that's probably a lot of your own shit."

Jane was right about one thing, some of this *was* my own shit, and it was on me to figure out and fix if I wanted to be with her. But how? I didn't even fully understand what I was feeling. Was it jealousy? Was it shame? What was so painful here? I needed to know, but it eluded me. I stayed in that other room for a good bit of time chatting with people till I felt it was safe to go back through and see Jane. I was shaken though.

***

Adding to the complexity of the balancing act I was doing was that Jane saw herself as something of an activist against entrenched sexist paradigms about women's sexual behavior. She would frequently post things on social media that were suggestive of her lifestyle, which was a test for me. Sitting down for some social media time to catch up on what friends were doing and getting blasted with posts about her nighttime hijinks was not uncommon. But when I was out of town, her posts had an even more devastating impact. Photos of her with other men in a context that made it clear what they were up to, or what my head said they were just about to be up to, were more than I wanted to deal with.

I learned to stay off social media while I traveled, but I don't live in a bubble, and invariably a friend would make some comment to me in conversation. "Oh, I saw that Jane was talking about [insert any random-night-out story]." They weren't trying to push my buttons or anything. I'm sure they just thought of it as scandalous and fun to talk about. They didn't know what I was going through.

These comments always came unexpectedly, popping up at what I was hoping was going to be a fun social evening with friends. There was no way to get away from it and it felt like there was no safe place to hide. I found myself engaged in a delicate balancing act.

While there was plenty in my life to be excited and happy about, my ability to continue in the relationship was predicated on my ability to ignore as much as I could about her physical attraction to other men and what she was doing while I was away. Intellectually, I knew that I had chosen to enter this minefield, and that navigating it was the whole point. But for the moment, the land mines were dangerous, and the hurt was real.

The time was coming when I was going to have to learn how to disarm them or just step on one after another in order to learn how to not be affected by it. In all honesty though, I know I was hoping that she would change, rather than my having to do all the growing up I'd told myself I wanted and needed. But changing her ways was not the path Jane was currently on and the inevitable collision of the unstoppable force meeting the immovable object was getting closer. The problem being that the immovable object had no idea what he was doing, and the unstoppable force knew precisely who she was and why.

***

Act II, Scene 75
Adam and Jane are home. It's evening.

JANE: Babe, I'm starting to get the feeling that you don't want to hear about my hookups. Why not?

ADAM: I guess I think that it's your business and I don't need to be part of it.

JANE: You're not interested in my life?

ADAM, *stammering*: No, it's not that. I'm only here half the time so I don't want to cloud the time we do have with these things. And to be perfectly straight with you, I'm still not entirely comfortable with it all.

JANE: Would you prefer that I didn't hook up with other guys?

ADAM: That would be an oversimplification of my thoughts. I want you to be you.

JANE: Okay, that's good. But the thing is, I really want to share my stories with you. I think it's hot and you're my partner, so I like feeling that you know all about me.

ADAM: I know that, and I'm trying to figure out how to be okay with it but haven't cracked the code yet.

JANE: Should I stop telling you them?

ADAM, *sighing*: No . . . the battle I have in my head about it is that if I continue to ignore it or ask you to keep it hidden so I can pretend it's not happening, then at some level I feel like I'm living a lie. I've told myself that's not how I want to live. Besides, it's actually causing me to dig deeper into myself to figure out where the emotions are coming from, and well, I enjoy that type of self-examination.

JANE: Okay, I guess we'll just continue on like this . . . until we don't.

The sharing was, in an odd way, a love language for Jane. It was one of the ways she expressed her intimacy toward me, but I wasn't able to recognize this at the time. It just felt like taking hits to the body, and the haphazard nature of how she initially shared her exploits was tough for me. She would frequently launch into a recap of an interlude at what I felt were very strange moments, such as when we were in bed about to watch a movie or having a nice dinner. When we were close, she saw it as a perfect opportunity for her to share and get closer, but the sharing would have the opposite effect on me. I'd be overwhelmed with negative emotions and my evening would take on a much more uncomfortable vibe, the exact opposite of her intention. I also had to hide the true intensity of the jealousy from Jane so that presented some challenges for me on how I was processing all these developments.

There was one big piece of data to this whole experiment that was always right in front of my face and impossible to ignore: Jane loved hearing about my hookups. She was never jealous of, nor intimidated by, the other women I had been with over the course of our relationship. That was significant to me and was something to aspire to.

But the balancing act that I was doing was getting harder and harder. I could feel an underlying current of fear when we were together—not knowing if a share about a hookup was going to come out of nowhere, not knowing when a text exchange would light her expression up. On top of that, I also had to hide "my own shit" from Jane, so I was bottling a lot up, which never ends well. This all came to a head on one particular evening.

It was my third night being home after a work trip out west. Jane and I had tickets to a new immersive theater experience based on *Alice in Wonderland* that we had been really looking forward to attending. We were having a great night out. After dinner at a funky new restaurant, we wandered around the industrial neighborhood in Brooklyn where the theater was.

The show was being performed in an old insane asylum from the early 1900s. Creepy as fuck, and they didn't need to do too much in the way of set building. Dust and cobwebs everywhere, stained dirty tiles, with old porcelain-covered cast-iron institutional sinks set into the walls. Each room was lit with a single dim filament bulb in a metal fixture dangling from the end of a thick black cord that emerged from the center of the cracked and peeling ceiling.

It was an intimate affair, with only fifteen audience members at each performance. We were seated in a waiting room as a woman in 19th-century dress stood at the front, giving us detailed instructions about what to expect and how to interact with the set and cast as they moved us around during the show. She asked if anyone was claustrophobic. She told us if there was an emergency at any point, we would need to let a cast member know so they could stop the show and escort us out. My anticipation was building and the whole thing was fantastic. It felt like this was going to be a theater experience like no other.

There was a pause while we waited for the show to start. I took Jane's hand in mine, and looking down at it, I noticed a leather bracelet around her wrist that I hadn't seen before. As I ran my fingers on it, she said, "Isn't that cool? I had a threesome a couple nights ago with these two guys and one of them was a designer. He makes them."

Instantly, I was totally out of control, brakes squealing, car flying off the road and sailing over a cliff. A second later the lights went out and the sound system of the theater came alive.

Holy fuck. Did that just happen? The show was beginning all around me, but I wasn't there anymore. My head was a million miles away and I had no idea how to deal with the situation I had been thrown into. Communication with Jane wasn't possible, taking a walk to collect my thoughts wasn't possible, and comprehending the show wasn't the possible. As the *Alice in Wonderland* characters appeared all around me, their masks and costumes took on a horrific quality. The walls, the shadows, the Mad Hatter, the White Rabbit, and the Caterpillar, they were all laughing at me. I was surrounded, in a nightmare, with the strangest creatures and characters yelling, laughing, dancing, talking. The audience got separated and ushered into several different rooms.

There was loud dialogue and music. It all was very confusing. The Cheshire Cat grabbed me and stuffed me in a closet. Were they all in cahoots against me? I turned around in the small space to see that the back of the closet had a window into another room, where I saw the Queen of Hearts talking to Alice. I couldn't focus on what they were saying—all that was running through my head was Jane's threesome. Who were these guys? All my bottled-up angst from the last few months felt like it was about to explode.

Shortly a secret door in the side of the closet opened and the rabbit pulled me into a very dimly lit corridor, which ended in a small dining room with some of the characters, and a number of the audience members seated around the table. The rabbit and I sat down at the two empty seats; Jane was sitting at the far end of the table from me. I realized just how angry I was when I saw her.

I wanted to stand up and yell at her: "Are you crazy? Why would you tell me that right before a performance when I have no opportunity to process? Why did you give me so much work to do at a moment I was so happy?"

But instead, I had to settle for the Mad Hatter telling Alice how rude she was while the tea was poured into the mess of unmatched china that littered the table. Finger sandwiches were served; the characters all seemed to be talking at once.

The pressure had reached a critical point, and I needed to release it somehow. It seemed impossible to keep watching and listening. The other option I had was to remove myself, but I had no idea where the door was at that point. I would have had to interrupt the show to say I needed to go. Talk about embarrassing yourself. Putting my fragility on display like that was not a bridge I was going to cross at that moment. I was trapped again, in over my head, drowning in all that was going on around me.

How was I this fragile? My entire life, I thought I had proven I was made of stone and steel, yet here was all this evidence to the contrary. My brain started going down into a wild death spiral as this line of thinking started building steam. Maybe everything I had thought about my strength and composure was false. I had been faking it all this time to everyone, and I truly was an impostor. I caught the spiral and reminded myself that my brain was fucking with me. I was physically safe. There was no need to panic. I wasn't on some remote wall without a rope, a thousand feet up with no way out and no move to make. Deep breath and exhale. The show continued.

While the night at the theater was an extreme example of how and when *not* to tell your husband about your frolics, in general there didn't ever seem to be a good time to do it so that it went well. I never seemed to be ready to hear it when Jane decided to bring it up.

***

At the end of our first year of living together it was painfully obvious I was in over my head. I was existing at the intersection of two distinct realities.

On the one hand, I was living with and, strangely, now married to the woman I wanted to be with, and our connection on many levels was getting deeper. On the other hand, my life was slowly morphing into a nonstop barrage of events like what happened at the theater and at the sex party.

It hurt to hear her stories, and it felt like more and more of my energy was being spent on keeping myself from being overcome by negative thoughts. The land mines were going off more frequently and managing my emotions in these situations was complicated. I wasn't sure what I was supposed to be feeling or what the correct course of action was. In all fairness to Jane, she didn't know either, as this relationship was uncharted territory for her too.

There was really no way to keep hiding from it, and it felt like there was no point of safety. The enjoyable, rewarding relationship that I had hoped I could create was slipping away from me. Personal growth was proving elusive. Every time I managed to regain my calm, chill-the-fuck-out nature, something else would come crashing down, upending me emotionally and sweeping me away. It was eerily similar to experiences I've had up in the mountains, when things start unraveling little by little, and each misstep, each ignored sign, each poorly navigated hazard, brings you closer and closer to a disaster.

Chapter 6
Cigarette Break

It's 5 a.m. and a beautiful, cold Colorado winter morning is unfolding. As the coffee is brewing, I pop a breakfast burrito in the microwave, then go load my split-board and backcountry gear into the truck. My relationship with Jane is in a downward spiral, and I'm damned if I can figure out a way to pull out of it. With 10 inches of fresh snow on the high peaks, it's a perfect time to go find solace and inspiration in the mountains.

I pour the coffee in a travel mug, stuff the burrito into my jacket pocket, and head out into the cold morning to my silent waiting truck. My feet are crunching in the snow, my breath visible with every exhalation. I climb in and shut the door with a loud thud. Sitting in the dark cab, I'm surrounded by the familiar cold, hard surfaces of the old pickup. This is the pause, that beautiful moment when everything is only a possibility, with my breathing as the only sound breaking the stillness of the cold, dark morning.

I jam the clutch down while turning the key in the ignition, and the four-liter engine roars to life. I am instantly transformed into adventure mode.

The painted lines of the road endlessly pass by the field of my headlights. Dawn starts to emerge in the eastern sky as the truck follows the winding roads up to the trailhead at 10,000 feet. I'm heading into the national forest to engage with the mountains, climb up some remote peak, and execute a ride down one of its snowy features. More important, it's where I find peace. It's a check-in to make sure I'm still in there and that I'm okay to keep going.

A sixty-minute drive brings me to the empty trailhead, where it's dead quiet and far colder. I put my gear on, split my snowboard into two awkward skis and begin the cross-country approach though the snowy wilderness. My destination is a steep 1,500-foot couloir, a ribbon of snow dropping off the summit of Flat Top Mountain, a 12,350-foot peak just off the Continental Divide in Rocky Mountain National Park.

As I leave the trailhead and the truck behind, my brain switches over to wilderness mode. Being surrounded by the snowy forest is the first step to the peace and solitude I'm craving. This environment brings me into the meditative state where I can find my center. The moment I leave the road and parking lot, my brain starts settling down to simpler thought processes.

The freshly fallen snow is light and fluffy, its softness creating a stark silence to the morning. There is no wind. The trees all have a frosting of snowflakes. I glide through the forest, slowly climbing in elevation, on my way to the remote lake at the bottom of the couloir.

Solo backcountry adventures are a different kind of experience, and being on a mountain that size all by yourself is a feeling like no other, a complex mixture of fear, exhilaration, and perspective, which at the end of the day's adventure brings about a peaceful euphoria. Feelings like that must be worked for, and I have put the time in. I have all the tools, skills, and experience I need to get where I'm headed.

Kick, glide, pole-push, kick, glide, pole-push. The only noise is the clacking of my boots in the bindings, as one leg goes in front of the other, over and over again, the skis silent in the deep, fresh powder, which means I'm going to have one hell of a ride down. There is no way to ride this mountain without climbing it first. There is no lift, no snowcat, no helicopter that can bring you up. Human power or nothing.

Kick, glide, kick, glide. The trees are getting shorter and spaced farther apart. I continue to gain elevation till I break tree line and feel the warmth of the rising sun on my body. The sunglasses come out. The sky is an impossible blue, the snow a pristine white, the mountains in sharp relief against the clear sky. I am now in church, and the sermon is beginning. I stop, and listen, and just stare.

This sight never fails to awe and inspire me. I now have the first look at my destination: a sharp white ribbon of snow splitting the dark rock face of the distant peak.

I continue, snaking my way up on a frozen creek, and in no time at all I am at a wide-open field of white that hides the frozen high alpine lake beneath it. A perfectly flat sheet of unbroken snow from last night's gentle storm, my tracks like a knife cut in the frosting of a cake as I head out across it to the couloir rising above it on the far side.

It's an uncharacteristically windless winter day, the air is perfectly still, the mountains hum and vibrate all around me, pumping peaceful energy into my body. I am the only moving thing up here. But I am now in the danger zone, where the environment can turn deadly in an instant and demands that I pay attention to the snow and signs of the natural terrain around me.

Reaching the far side of the lake, I stop and stare straight up at the top of the peak. Balanced above me at an angle of 50 degrees is 1,500 feet of pristine, unbroken snow in a perfect sheet. Each snowflake weighs a millionth of an ounce, but if they join forces and decide to slide, I'd be crushed beneath them, as dead as those rocks off to my right. But I know they won't. I know this mountain. I know how it moves, how it breathes. I have spent years getting to know each of these peaks around me. As a cocky young man, I thought I could take anything that came at me. I made mistakes and was lucky to come out okay. But each time I got knocked down by these mountains, I learned from the experience.

There's an old climbing adage, "The mountain doesn't care." It doesn't care if you live or die, or even if you're there. The mountain is just being its authentic mountain self. Sometimes it's throwing shit at you. Rocks and large ice blocks will fall; avalanches can come screaming at you; weather comes in and beats you down, sometimes trapping you till it passes. These things aren't personal—and they're part of the allure and challenge of climbing in an extreme environment. The bigger the climb, or the further away from civilization you are, the greater the potential for things to become very complicated if you mishandle a situation. That's why the most valuable lesson I learned from the mountains was how to maintain the calm and calculating state I call the climber's mindset.

When I started scrambling on rocks as a kid in Central Park, it wasn't supercritical to have my head in the right place. But when I graduated to technical types of climbing, the mindset started to become an increasingly important factor in my safety and success. My high level of energy, which served me well in so many ways, was a liability when I was trying to focus on difficult terrain, especially when something went wrong.

A climbing mentor once told me that the first thing I needed to do when a critical problem came up was take out a cigarette and smoke it while I thought it through. He didn't mean that literally, of course. The point was, rather than reacting to a situation immediately, I needed to train myself to pause and analyze it from several different angles. That conflicted with my natural instinct to jump right in and do something. Learning to stay calm when a world of shit is going on around me has certainly saved my life on more than one occasion.

As my climbing got better and I started free soloing, this calm mindset became the difference between life and death.

But the most critical lesson I've had to learn is giving things the respect they deserve. When I've ignored that rule in the mountains, it has almost killed me. My worst fail at this was many years ago on a free solo. I was a good way up a rock face that I knew was well within my climbing ability, but I wasn't giving the climb the respect it deserved. Even though it was an easy climb for me, a fall would have been fatal, so I needed to respect that and take what I was doing seriously. Whether it was ego or overconfidence, I had a lack of focus, causing me to slip off the rock, a good sixty feet above the boulder-strewn ground.

It was only dumb luck that saved me: a piece of equipment I was carrying on my climbing harness just happened to catch on a bit of rock, stopping my fall. I was left hanging there, staring at the tiniest nub of rock that made the difference between living and dying. As I stared at where the equipment had hooked on the rock, I literally saw my life flash before my eyes. Not giving that climb the respect it deserved may have been the dumbest thing I have ever done, and I nearly paid the ultimate price. A shiver goes through my body whenever I think of that day.

Climbing taught me that if I let go of ego, respect the mountain, and take the time to learn the environment, I could start to understand how the mountain lives and breathes, and how best to coexist with it. If you want the elation, joy, and ecstasy of coexisting with the mountain, you have to acknowledge and accept all the hazards that come with it, and make sure you have the knowledge, the skills, and a plan to navigate those hazards. Plain and simple, you must balance seeking the risk with giving the mountain the respect it deserves.

The mountains are where I learned focus. The mountains are where I learned how to train my body and brain for difficult goals. The mountains taught me that when I get out of my comfort zone and embrace the risk, that's where the true learning is. That's why I started free soloing. There is a simple beauty in climbing without a rope, or diving without a tank, or skydiving without an airplane (BASE jumping). It's a way of keeping myself out of the comfort zone and challenging myself physically and mentally.

Through these challenges, I have a chance to see just what forces are in play inside me, and with a calm and calculating mindset I can address those forces and achieve great things. This is where I grew up. So why the fuck aren't these life lessons working for my relationship with Jane? I couldn't be more out of my comfort zone in parts of this journey with her. I break the silence with a yell, which echoes off the peaks and fades away. No response—the mountain doesn't care.

This perfect slope of snow above me isn't going to snowboard itself, so I take the split boards off my feet, snap them together to form my snowboard, strap it to my pack, and begin the steep climb.

Signs of Stability vs. Signs of Instability

The snow is deeper up here. I step up and sink in, step up and sink in, over and over and over again. After thirty minutes of high output on Mother Nature's StairMaster, I pause, letting it all settle. As my breathing starts to relax a little, I turn to look behind me and see the snow-covered frozen lake below me, much smaller now, with a trail of footprints leading from it up to me. I begin to feel the steepness and the height.

I take this moment to assess the environment again. I know that this couloir, due to its orientation compared to the top ridge of the mountain, doesn't get extra snow loaded on it from the wind. I also know that the regular high winds in this area prevent snow hoar from building up on the surface of the slope, which could otherwise become a slide layer. I know that last night's storm came in wet at first before turning cold, so the new snow bonded well to the existing slope. These are all signs of stability which allow me to feel safe.

The problem is, you can *always* find signs of stability on *any* slope, and if you only focus on them while ignoring or minimizing the signs of instability, you may find yourself in a dangerous situation that was totally avoidable. The cardinal rule for playing in avalanche terrain is you must look for the signs of instability.

Has there been any localized snow movement caused by my travel? Have I experienced any sounds of the slope settling as I stomp up it, like any hollowness or whumping? As I step does my foot hit a weak layer and all of a sudden sink further in, or is there consistent resistance to my weight? Do I see any long cracks as I break the surface tension with my steps? Are there any obvious signs of natural slide activity in the area?

I stop and stare up at the remaining slope above me, which is slightly intimidating when you're in the middle of an ocean of balanced snow, and especially when you're alone. I drink in the intimidation and the fear, and it feels good. There is no such thing as being 100 percent safe, at least not on any slope that you'd want to ski.

That was something that took years to absorb, that the intimidation and fear of the mountains was the whole point. When I was younger, I thought the point was to be able to say, "I climbed that," and whatever fear I felt was an obstacle in the way of the trophy. But now the adventures were interesting because of that fear, not in spite of it.

I continue my upward progress. The couloir begins to narrow in the last 500 feet and now I'm in the most dangerous part of the climb. Cliffs tower above me on each side to wall me in. Speed is safety here because the cold cliffs are being hit with direct sunlight. As they warm, they have the potential to send rocks down into the couloir and in this last 500 feet, I have nowhere to hide. Stopping here is the most dangerous thing I could do. I have to keep moving, either up toward the summit or back down toward the lake. Those are the only safe options now.

I continue upward. The snow ends at a steep incline of rocks. A short climb up them, about 100 feet or so, can take me to the summit, which I generally don't care about, as I usually want to get to the snowboarding, but I'm feeling like I need some inspiration. I'm looking for a sign and the summit seems as likely a place to find one as any.

I drop my pack here, as it would just be dead weight, but make sure to grab my small thermos of coffee and stuff it in a pocket. Putting my gloved hands on the rock, I scramble up the short climb and break out of the couloir to gain the wide summit. I face the sun, close my eyes, and sink into the peace of this moment. The thin air is gloriously fresh. The lightest breath of wind brushes my cheeks.

The mountains, the snow, the vast vault of blue sky. Time stands still. I stand still, eyes closed. Peace. I just stand there and absorb the natural world, with deep breaths in through my nose and out through my mouth. I can feel the massive power of the mountain, its gravitational pull solidly connecting me to its summit as if energy were flowing through my legs, both firmly planted on the hard granite. I open my eyes. I see snowcapped mountains in every direction, the sun beaming at me, still well below its apex, letting me know it's morning on a mountaintop. I am alive; I am in love with life. This is the check-in. This is how I know I'm still there.

I take out the thermos and have myself a hot coffee on the summit. I'm happy, I'm focused, I'm in my calm climber's mindset. It occurs to me that I've been relying on this mindset too heavily in my relationship with Jane, thinking that as long as I kept my cool and took time to think about the situation, I'd figure my way through it.

In reality though, I've been finding myself on shakier and shakier ground, and I definitely haven't been "figuring it out." And though I've been able to maintain a calm demeanor, on the inside, I've been moving from emotional crisis to emotional crisis. I've been just as reckless as I was as a cocky young man, thinking I could handle anything the mountain threw at me.

I think back to that free solo where I nearly fell to my death. What saved me? A nub of rock, dumb luck, no skill or depth of experience there. I hadn't given that climb the respect it deserved, and I saw I was making the same mistake in my relationship with Jane.

I look at the summit I'm standing on. A wide span of granite the size of a football field. The journey to get up here this morning was a complex dance with risk, desire, and experience. Even so, it wasn't stressful because I know what I'm doing. I've learned how I operate, what I'm capable of, and I intimately know the environment I'm operating in. I respect the mountain and all its inherent risks, I have plans in place to minimize those risks, and emergency procedures in case something unexpected comes up. If a hazard comes at me, it's part of the deal, it's part of the environment, it's part of the risk I'm seeking, and I have the experience to handle it.

Maybe I need to start taking the same approach in my relationship. The hazards were coming so fast that I never had a chance to reflect on the internal cause of my reactions. Maybe I need to plan more. Maybe I need to be as calculating in my navigation of the hazards when I'm with Jane in the city as I am when I'm alone in the backcountry. As much as I care about Jane, as much as I care about our relationship, looking back at how I've been operating, I realize that I haven't recognized the true impact of what I agreed to. I realize that I haven't been giving this journey the respect it deserves.

Playing in the mountains at elite levels requires a remarkable amount of training, preparation, analysis, and thought. Beyond the physical skills, you have to be clear with yourself about what you're doing and why. I know I had this conversation with myself when I chose to enter into the relationship. It was one of the central tenets underlying that decision—that the risks I take must fit in with the larger context of what I want my life to be. Entering into an open relationship or climbing a difficult mountain only makes sense if it's something I really want to do. It would be foolish to seek that kind of a risk if the experience itself wasn't very important to me. Do I want to be in an open relationship? Do I want to be in *this* open-as-fuck relationship?

The problem is, I constantly feel like I'm about to fall, and that's an awful way to live. But what would our relationship be like if it didn't feel that way? What would a beautiful summit look like on this journey? I could feel the dead weight of emotional baggage that was preventing me from finding out. This feeling of standing on the summit of Flat Top Mountain, could I get to a similar place on this journey with Jane?

But to get to *that* summit, I have some big challenges in front of me. I'll be thrown into risky situations that could have long-term effects on me if they aren't addressed properly. I probably can't even fathom all the things I'm going to be presented with on this journey. How am I going to become familiar with this emotional terrain while at the same time keeping myself safe enough to continue, and not get destroyed by it?

Dealing with my emotional responses to Jane's sexual connections has proven to be far more serious a matter than I was prepared for. But if I had some space, some breathing room, perhaps I could begin to let go of the ego, which is the growth I'm seeking. The ego drives trophy-bagging behavior; the ego pushes back against the risks that threaten it. But the more I sink into those risks and let go of the bravado, the easier the journey would become. Now this is feeling like familiar ground: it all starts with acknowledging the risks and giving them the respect they deserve.

Somehow, I have to be more calculating about engaging with the risks. I have to make sure I'm prepared for the dangerous emotions when they arise and think of them as part of the deal, not as an aberration.

I sip my coffee and start wandering around the summit, looking down at my booted feet as I walk. Jane needs to share her stories with me. It's something I casually agreed to, but it has been wrecking me. Engaging with her at that level is basically a free solo up some rock face and I've been treating it like it's no big deal. This is new territory for me, and I should have had a serious discussion with her about how to navigate it. Instead, I've been winging it, relying on my mindset to carry me through, trying to seem strong and confident, and hoping I would be able to figure it out along the way.

I can see nearly the entire 514 square miles of Rocky Mountain National Park spread out all around me. I can see countless summer climbing and winter snowboarding adventures in any direction I look. I can see easier routes Jane and I climbed together, harder routes that my climbing partner and I ascended, and places we explored, looking for a never-before-discovered line.

A mountain in the distance reminds me of the free solo many years ago when fear got the better of me halfway up the climb and I had to turn back, unable to continue, unable to reframe the experience, unable to manage the emotions. It had been a day of failure on many levels.

In a different direction, I see the three granite spires, each over a thousand feet tall, that my climbing partner and I had climbed in a fifteen-hour day. We trained all summer to do that, and we were at the top of our game back then. We were an unstoppable team. But that didn't just happen from day one. We had to learn to work together at building skills and learn to let go of ego and bravado. Learning how to work together with another person like that taught me more about life than almost anything else.

When we were training for climbs—climbs on which our lives would be dependent on each other—we would meet weekly to discuss our progress. This allowed us to have a place to admit to our failings, talk about our successes, and generally check in and connect with each other. Any important issues that arose would be discussed at this meeting, not out in the field.

What if I suggest to Jane that we use this framework as a way for us to share any of the extracurriculars that take place while we are apart? It would be a deliberate conversation, giving her a chance to share everything she wanted to say, but in a structured time and place.

That would give me the breathing room I need. It would allow me to focus and be better prepared to handle my reactions in the moment, and eventually identify what was causing them. The more I think about it, the more I like this idea. I wouldn't keep getting taken by surprise, which never gave me a good, grounded place to work on "my own shit." Instead, I'd have the time to prepare mentally; I would go in knowing I was about to hear difficult things. Equally important, it would show Jane I was giving her needs the respect they deserved and finding a way to accommodate them.

But what would Jane think of all this? There's an added challenge. She's demonstrated pretty clearly that she doesn't want to deal with my emotional difficulties surrounding our open relationship. She's been completely self-absorbed in her own desires regarding sex and seems to be devoid of feelings about these concerns. I really wish Jane could be a little more empathetic about my emotions—but that's her shit to work on. On the other hand, she heard me out and agreed to only have sex with other people when I'm out of town, which from her point of view is a major lifestyle compromise. We're partners, and it seems like I'll need to broach the subject with her as a way to get us both what we need and what we want.

I wander around the summit for a few more minutes turning this idea over in my head. I want to keep on this journey, I want to stay in this relationship, I want to continue seeking the risk. I know there's baggage that I'm carrying around. This relationship is exposing so much I was unaware of. It's opening a window into my ego and into my soul. I'm looking for the changes that this journey will produce, which is exactly what I've been failing to achieve so far. I'm not going to admit defeat until I've exhausted all possible avenues of success.

I walk slowly back to the top of the couloir and begin the careful down climb to my waiting gear. Reaching my pack and board at the top of the snow, I'm in the cold shadows again. The snow all around me is perfect. I feel like an intruder in this quiet place.

I unbuckle the straps holding my snowboard to the pack and carefully stick it in the snow. I strap the goggles on my helmet and fold up my poles to stuff them in my bag. I swing my pack onto my back, strap it tight to my body, and carefully expose the rip cord for the avalanche balloon, the Hail Mary option to save my life if the slope releases on my way down and I'm caught in a slide.

I carefully lay the board down in the small platform I've carved out for myself and gingerly step into the bindings, snapping them shut. Standing up straight on the board perpendicular to the fall line, my back to the slope, I look out at the mountains across the vast space above the lake, and then down at the perfect snow slope below me. The flat snow can be hard to read, so my attention goes to the line of footprints off to the side leading all the way down to the lake, helping me gauge the angle and the depth.

It's steep. A 50-degree slope doesn't sound like much until you're standing on the top of it. I'm alive with fear, exhilaration, and anticipation. Sunglasses off, goggles down over my eyes, and a long exhale.

The pause. The moment when all the kinetic energy is still in it its potential form, and everything is still a possibility, not an actuality. There is nothing in my world but this steep slope of snow and me on my snowboard. The focus takes hold. All other cares, worries, and pleasures fall away. I am one with the mountain and the environment. The moment comes to an end and with a strong inhale, I hop up, twist my body so the board points downhill, and I'm off.

Picking up speed, carving back and forth, the snowboard floating on the heavenly powder, I'm free. The wind whips past my ears, and the cliff walls fly by as I execute giddy turns on the journey down. Floating, bobbing up and down with each carve, sprays of snow going high in the air, the loose snow I release racing me down the mountain on either side of my line. Focusing on all that is going on with the ride, reading each turn before executing it, looking for any indication of rocks under the surface, making sure the sliding snow is only surface sluff and not an indication of a greater danger. Turn after turn after turn, too numerous to count.

In the last 150 feet, I straighten out my ride and point the board straight down toward the lake, picking up speed to see how far I can get across it before losing my momentum. Flying in a crouch position, I hit the flat expanse of the lake in a huge poof of snow. Instantly my speed starts dropping, the board sinking deeper and deeper until I come to a stop about a third of the way across.

Peace. Pure satisfaction. My god, the feeling I get after a drop like that is indescribable. Sometimes there is no substitute for doing something that allows you to feel like a badass motherfucker, even if it's only to yourself.

Stepping out of my bindings and sinking into the deep snow on the lake, I turn around and trace the course of the wiggly line as it eventually morphs into a straight one and ends right at me. The only sound is that of my breathing echoing under my helmet. Inhale and exhale, inhale and exhale. I admire the elegant design I have painted on the surface of the snow, and then look up toward the summit where I had been standing a short time ago.

I'm hopeful that I still have loads to give in fighting for this relationship. I haven't been beaten by it. I'm still just figuring it out. Like any new skill or sport, I need to take it one step at a time.

I turn to head back to the trailhead. It has been a brilliant morning. I walk across the lake, dragging my board like some sullen teenager and then have a smooth, easy ride down through the trees to the road and my waiting truck. Even with all the time I spent on the summit, I'm still going to be in the office by 10:30 am.

***

A day or two later I spoke to Jane on the phone about how I wanted us to start sharing our experiences in a controlled space. I acknowledged her needs and that I understood how important (and fun) it was for her to share those experiences. It wasn't the easiest thing for me, I admitted, but I wanted to find a way to be that partner for her. I needed a deliberate, structured environment for this, which would allow me to give her stories the focus that she wanted—and help me learn how to be a willing participant.

"We could cook dinner and make a night of it," she said.

I was pleased to see that she was excited about it and pitching in right away to make it something that was both of ours. The only thing she wanted to know was when. A totally valid question that I hadn't really considered. Laughing together, we acknowledged the first night home was generally a hot and steamy affair we wouldn't want to disrupt and waiting too long might defeat the whole purpose of releasing tension on both our parts. We agreed the most logical solution seemed to be the second night after I got back. It would also give me the day to prepare mentally for whatever she might say. The tough work would be compartmentalized, and she would no longer surprise me with something at an inopportune moment.

I spent the remainder of my trip out west in a lighter place. All the new snow we were getting certainly helped keep my spirits up too and I spent a good number of days out playing with my adventure buddies on some wild rides. It was good to be alive.

Chapter 7
Time to Get to Work

Ten days later, I flew home and the day after that, the first deliberate share time had come. As per normal for us after three weeks apart, the previous night and that morning had been a fuckfest of grand proportions. This, as you would expect, always put me in a relaxed state, but I knew that in the evening I was going to be hearing about her hookups, so underneath my calm exterior there were significant notes of apprehension. I didn't know if I would be able to do it.

I was uneasy but committed to this. The million-dollar question in my mind was would it bring us closer together, or would it accelerate the breakup? This was leaning into the risk in a way I had never anticipated. Here we were, just after finishing dinner in our apartment, dirty dishes in the sink, and about to cross the Rubicon.

I was sitting in the living room when Jane came over with the bottle and refilled my empty wine glass. She sat down next to me, each of us with an arm over the back of the Ikea couch, opposite legs crossed so we could face each other. With a big smile on her face, she settled into the cushions. Her eyes were sparkling, her body relaxed and elegant. And then she began recounting the three different hookups she had had while I was away.

One of the hookups was a two-guy threesome, which she seemed to manifest with impressive frequency. Probably every other month during those years, and only about half of those included me. As she began going into detail, the room, the sofa, the wine, and coffee table all disappeared, and my tunnel vision centered on Jane. It felt like every nerve in my body had come alive.

Jane had been chatting with one of the guys online through a hookup app when she asked if he could bring a friend along, which, surprisingly, he agreed to. They met in a bar, where Jane made them lift up their shirts up to verify that the photos they had sent of their abs were current. After confirmation, and then a quick drink together, Jane suggested they move to the nearby apartment of one of the men, which they were slightly shocked by. For some reason, I do enjoy hearing how guys she meets who don't know her are slightly thrown off by a woman who is as sexually forward as Jane is. They both kept remarking that they hadn't ever met anyone like her before. Welcome to the club, gentlemen.

As she got more into the story, she sat up on the edge of couch, making eye contact with me as I was leaning back, focusing on me with an energetic intensity as she talked.

In what turned out to be a stunningly beautiful apartment, after a fairly intense make-out session in the living room, she got their clothes off and began going to work on both them with her mouth and hands, getting them ready for the pleasure she was desiring. I could feel the conflict in my brain between being aroused by a woman who loved performing oral sex this much and the reality of hearing about it in this context.

The group moved to the lush bedroom and even with all her effort, one of the guys was having a tough time staying hard. I could see her disappointment when she relayed that a double penetration, which was her holy grail of threesomes, was not going to be possible. She was going to have to settle for an alternative. A slight wave of satisfaction ran through me at hearing that, but it was quickly extinguished as she described the ensuing scene.

With the candlelight flickering in the room, she caught a glimpse of the three of them in the mirror, her on all fours, bright white skin between the two ripped black men on their knees, one in front of her, one behind her, and it was that glimpse in the mirror that sent her into shuddering orgasm.

My pulse was pounding in my head, not that this type of behavior was a revelation to me, but there was something about the fact that it had happened three days ago, and that I was hearing about it in such stark detail, that was so raw and new and intense for me. This was obviously bringing her closer in but was it pushing me away at the same time?

I couldn't really think about that yet as I was doing everything I could to be present and listen—not just wait for her to finish so I could get and up pretend to drink tea, but truly listen. Listen to her describe in detail the feeling of the four hands on her body.

Listen to her describe the smoothness of their cocks. Listen to her describe the intensity of her own orgasm.

"Thank you, Sir. May I have another?" is the thought that went through my head as she finished the first story. I knew there were two more coming, so I had to lean in.

Of the three hookups she described that evening, two of them came from the apps but the third one started at a café with a couple of friends, and oddly, this is the one that stung the most. They had been finishing lunch when a guy came up to her and gave her his number, saying he had seen her and really wanted to ask her out. She went on and on about how bold she thought he was, so she called, they had a drink together, and it ended with her bringing him home.

She finished the last story, and it was over. I didn't really have much to say yet. We just kind of shrugged, smiled, and sat there for a moment.

"How was that?"

"Hmm, not sure yet. Let me process and I'll get back to you on it," I said with an air of tension.

"Of course. Thanks for giving it a try. It meant a lot and was pretty great for me. I've never really had a situation where I could do that deliberately before."

Jane finished the last sip of wine from her glass and got up to clean the dishes. I walked into the bedroom to put the laundry away.

As I sat there folding laundry, I found myself still thinking about that third hookup. Why had it bothered me so much more?

Was it that she thought he was so bold? She's married to me and she thinks *that's* bold? Was I feeling unseen in *my* boldness? That was part of it, but the more I thought about it, I realized the thing that really got me was that while the first two were deliberate decisions to go have a hookup, the fact that the other one started randomly—as others had, on subway platforms, at the theater, on an airplane or bus ride—is what left me with an uneasy feeling. It was a reminder that anytime, anywhere, Jane was always open to an invitation from someone she found hot enough to fuck.

It was this idea that continually haunted me.

Was it that I interpreted it as her being unsatisfied with me? Or was it that I desired her to sometimes just bask in our bond to the point of not always needing or wanting other sex partners? Was this something I was going to need to address with her? But how would I even approach that? Suggest a rule that pickup apps were okay, but organically meeting someone when she was out and about wasn't? It sounded almost comical. Perhaps I was never going to get comfortable with her constant desire for the next sexual experience, and it would cause me to move on if she wouldn't or couldn't change. I needed to be clear with myself that it was very possible I was not going to be able to meet Jane where she wanted but until I reached that point, I was going to keep trying.

Sitting there that evening, even with time to prepare, it was not any easier to hear the stories. I wouldn't say it went well, but when it was over, it was over, and for the rest of my time at home I knew I wasn't going to be surprised by having to process a hookup at an inopportune moment. I wasn't sure how I felt about the experience, but I could see it meant a lot to Jane. It was her way of getting closer to me and I could feel that, but more important she saw that I was willing to engage with her and take part in something that was meaningful to her.

It was hard to think of this as a win, given how difficult it was, but that night, when I walked into the bedroom, I looked at Jane and she looked at me. I can't really say what it was, but something had changed, and when I climbed into bed, she put her arm around me, and laid her head on my chest. It felt very real and close.

This whole experience was showing me what it's like when two people try to be together because they want the connection and are willing to compromise, to do what it takes to make it happen.

The next morning when I woke up, I opened my eyes and stared at the ceiling. I could hear Jane's breathing in my left ear, and I turned to look at her. Asleep next to me, on her stomach with her face pointed my way, she was so peaceful. As I lay there with her, I saw how everything in the room told some part of our story. The curtains and cheap furniture we had bought before the recent success of my company, her scarves hanging from the hooks I'd mounted on the wall. I remembered the fascination I'd had when she asked me to put them up. "How many scarves?" I asked, not sure I had heard her correctly when she had said, "Thirty or forty."

Sitting on top of the dresser was the rack of earrings and necklaces that she wore, an eclectic group of items that were evidence of her funky artistic taste and her modest academic life. I don't think the woman owned anything that was brand named unless it was purchased at a thrift store. Her elegance and style were the kind you can't buy; they were expressions of the confidence she exuded.

I slowly eased myself out of bed and quietly closed our bedroom door behind me. As the espresso machine heated up, I had a lightness in me I had not felt since the very beginning of moving in together.

I sat at the dining table with my coffee and got to work at my list of bugs and coding issues. The software I had developed over the past couple years was now running strong for a good and growing client base. As I was sitting there, flying through the lines of code, I was overcome with a feeling of satisfaction. I had been building something and now it was starting to come to fruition. The most enjoyable thing for me was getting my hands dirty. A social studies teacher in high school once told me that if I insisted on doing the work myself, I'd never be rich. He was right, but the trade-off of being completely removed from the creative process, was always too much for me and it's not like I'm poor. I'm just not at the point where I'm flying business class everywhere. These few hours each morning were gold to me, uninterrupted time to get some good work done at home.

Like clockwork, almost two hours to the minute after I had woken up, I got the text from Jane, a single emoticon of a coffee cup. She was awake, so I prepared two coffees to bring into the bedroom, the start of our morning ritual, which ended up being particularly wonderful that day.

The new framework for sharing Jane's exploits began to relieve a fairly serious hazard in our relationship. I was more relaxed in our day-to-day life when I was home. These stories became a deliberate event that I was a part of, rather than a random thing that was just happening to me that I had not fully bought into. Adding that little bit of structure improved both of our lives.

We got into a good rhythm and I felt like I had stopped the death spiral our relationship seemed to be in. Even though it felt to me like I was soaring, I was completely unaware of how much more I needed to do to get back up to a good cruising altitude.

> *Excerpt from Adam's journal (continued):*
> *Bam!!* I feel the power of the impact as the avalanche slams into my body, tossing me like a rag doll into the void. I'm in free fall, tumbling. My world has gone completely abstract. "Fuuuck" is the thought that goes through my head.
>
> After the initial shock subsides, a calm focus takes hold. I take in all that is going on around me, and to me. I notice that my body is sort of continually bumping on a hardish surface: Okay, that's interesting. Tumbling, tumbling, tumbling,

along with thousands of pounds of snow and ice. I review what's going on with each of my limbs, which seem to be still functioning, and I also realize I still have one of my ice axes in my hand. Putting a few things together, I understand that I am under the avalanche as we're flying down the mountain and that hardish surface is the slide layer of the slope. The years of training kick in and taking as much control of the situation as possible, I flatten out my body to stop the tumbling and roll over onto my ice axe. With the full weight of my body behind it, I drive the pick into the hard sliding surface of snow. I quickly come to a stop as the avalanche continues down the mountain without me. A second later my partner hits the end of the rope and I'm dragged a couple more feet down, but the axe holds in the steep, firm snow. I'm alive, but still a long way from safety.

Chapter 8
Digging Deeper into the Toolbox

A few months later, I was on my own in the apartment, trying to get some work done, and found myself somewhat dreading that evening's sharing activity. I'd gotten back from a trip the day before, and I didn't like how uncomfortable I was with what was coming. It was clear I had more to figure out around it.

I stood up and went to the espresso machine. What was I feeling? What was going on? I recognized the emotions of jealousy and fear swirling around in my head. I thought about that first sex party we had been at, when I walked into the room and saw Jane on the bed with the three guys. I had to turn away. I was scared of what might bubble up inside me if I really looked at what was happening. Like any number of the times I had backed off a climb or snowboarding drop when fear got the better of me. The problem becomes acute when the fear in question is out of proportion to the actual risk. Backing off in a situation like that, an unwarranted retreat, can do real damage to my self-confidence. And self-confidence is what's needed to perform at peak levels when you're at the edge of safety.

But being overwhelmed by fear when I'm out on the edge of some adventure is a fairly normal occurrence. I'm sure there are climbers who don't have any fear but I'm not one of them. When I'm hanging on to the rock face and contemplating my next move, being able to manage fear effectively can mean the difference between a good outcome and a bad one.

I've experienced the death spiral that fear can put me in enough times that it's easy for me to recognize. I'm attuned to it. It sets off physical changes in my body. I start emitting a strong odor, my heart rate goes up, my vision tunnels, my breathing gets shorter. My imagination conjures up all the possible negative futures that could happen. These unwanted visualizations can have a paralyzing effect—for example when I'm free soloing and feel like I can't make the next move without falling. The consequences of that negative thinking can be unpleasant, even fatal.

This is the sort of dangerous terrain where I call upon the "self-hypnosis reframe." Figuring out how to reframe or compartmentalize fear, to put it aside so it doesn't affect my decision-making, was one of the most difficult lessons I've had to learn in my lifetime of adventuring. How do I prevent fear, and negative visualizations of a possible future, from affecting the quality of my decision-making and performance in the present?

So there I am, on my fingertips and toes, clinging to a wall of rock, when I recognize that my brain has started to go down into a death spiral of fear. First, I tell myself to chill the fuck out and repeat the word "chill" a few times smoothly, almost like some sort of mantra. Then I begin my reframe. I tell myself that it's not fear I'm feeling but exhilaration at the amazing experience I'm having.

I think about how beautiful the view is and how lucky I am to be able to exist in this incredible environment. I visualize myself from above, on the majestic mountain with a stunning landscape stretched out behind me. That counter-visualization has the immediate effect of slowing my heart rate and focusing my mind on the task at hand.

By reframing the situation, I'm able to enter into a much better place emotionally and increase my enjoyment of the moment—not to mention decrease my chances of dying, which is really the main objective.

I realized that when emotion had gotten the better of me that night at the sex party, I hadn't even considered trying to reframe. I just kept walking. What would a reframe even look like in that kind of a situation? I also wondered why the other side of my brain hadn't dared me into staying and watching, which it often does when I'm faced with something that makes me uncomfortable. Maybe it had been just too much, a complete overload of the system.

I decided that I needed to think about our share time as an emotional free solo. I sipped my coffee. Why had that never occurred to me before? Could I go through the same mental processes, the same sort of reframing, to combat all the negative emotions and fantasies? Could I tell myself what an incredible life I'm having. Here is an amazing woman, who's living an amazing life, and she is sharing her life with me because it makes her happy to do so. Could I switch our roles in my head and think about all the wonderful experiences I've had that she has been supportive of? Like the fact that I had had a sexual encounter with another woman at that party not long before I walked into that room. Could I see our life from above, in the amazing environment of New York City, and see that this was extreme living at a vibration I had never thought possible?

Could reframing get me into a better place so I could listen to her stories with inquisitiveness and wonder? Could I listen to her stories in a way that brings me closer in? Could reframing make it at least possible to watch my wife get fucked by three men?

Standing there in the kitchen and going through this mental exercise was stressful. I was trying to find a way to get more engaged with something that could really damage me emotionally. I didn't have to do this; I could back off and walk away. There were plenty of times in my life when I've felt good about backing off, which always means you are alive to go adventuring on another day.

But there was so much about *this* adventure I was on with Jane that *was* satisfying. If I could successfully reframe the experience of hearing her stories and get comfortable with them, I was going to be able to continue going down this path with her. There was a lot at stake that was precious to me, and the difference between success and failure might be a life worth living.

That night, when Jane and I and sat down to begin sharing, I started going through the mental reframing process to relax myself, just as if I were climbing: Look at this amazing woman I am living with, who wants to get closer to me by sharing her stories. Look at this amazing life I am having. I reminded myself of the wonderful sexual experiences I'd recently had. I reminded myself of the fantastic threesomes with other women that Jane had helped arrange for us. I reminded myself of all the crazy sexual moments I'd had with her, and that these experiences were only possible because of who Jane was.

The effects were noticeable. The tunnel vision I normally had was comparatively mild. I was able to react to certain things with comments and engage with Jane conversationally. At one point I asked her how she felt when a guy had made a judgment about her sexuality with an off-color comment.

I got through the sharing session, and while it wasn't a perfect experience, it was better than before, a step in the right direction. It still took an emotional toll on me, but I did feel that I was getting closer to what Jane desired.

Over the next few months, I kept at it, using my tools, reframing, listening. I was managing to be a partner in this experiment, but the toll was cumulative and real. Jane was getting closer because of the effort, but at what cost to me? I didn't really feel like I was growing. It seemed more like I was just getting used to it, which in itself was good, but I could tell there was more going on with me.

Yes, I could listen to her stories now, but the fact that there was so much other sex going on was still taking me down. I wondered if maybe it was time to back off "the climb" of this relationship. The question was, Was this a warranted retreat or the kind where it was going to erode my confidence going forward?

This conflict of whether to retreat or not always brings up one day in particular. I was free soloing high up on a rock face, six miles from the trailhead, climbing at an elevation of thirteen thousand feet, when all of a sudden my confidence evaporated. I was certain I would pitch off into the void, smashing my body into the rocks far below. The moves were somewhat complex but should have been well within my ability. I just couldn't get my head in the right place. I was scared and saw myself in free fall, hurtling to my death. The death spiral of fear was taking hold, and I had to short-circuit it to continue the climb.

Standing on that ledge, staring at the rock in front of me, I started going through the mental exercises to put the fear in its place. After telling myself to chill the fuck out, I made a conscious effort to relax my body, letting my neck, back, and arms release the tension they had been holding. Then I closed my eyes and began my reframe, trying to replace the fear with positive emotions.

After running through my process, I opened my eyes on that ledge of rock and confidently got back to the climbing. But as I pulled up, my confidence evaporated, and the wave of fear completely enveloped me again. I tried to push, but my brain was convinced I was going to fall if I made the next move. This cycle repeated itself two more times before I concluded I was beaten.

I ended up sitting there for a while, just staring out into the valley below me, before I realized that trying to continue climbing with the reframe had a good chance of killing me. I had to back off, feeling defeated and freaked out at my mental failure, my confidence diminished, but alive to climb another day. On that climb I knew I was physically capable of executing the next step; I knew it was within my ability; I knew I wanted the experience of this climb. But for some reason, it was just too much, and I wasn't able to contain the fear of falling, which meant I probably would have fallen if I had tried. I couldn't safely continue, and some of my confidence in my soloing ability was lost that day.

Retreating from Jane was always an option. But I questioned what benefit backing off of this relationship would get me. Staying at it was going to be painful but I wasn't risking my life or grave physical harm, and staying at it could result in some breakthrough. I needed to get to a place where listening to Jane's exploits had a minimal emotional impact on me. I needed to not just recognize, but actually feel that it wasn't about me. If I could get to that state, perhaps I could eventually start enjoying it. That would be fantastic. It was a lofty goal, but pushing myself was why I was here, so continue I did.

Sitting in our apartment one evening, getting ready for a share session, I happened to be particularly relaxed. This may have been due to Jane's wearing a thong as she cleaned up after dinner. Her doing the cleaning was a normal occurrence, as I usually did the cooking, but on that night she had spilled wine on her jeans during dinner and had taken them off to soak. I was on the couch with a drink in hand, watching her float around the kitchen in her underwear and midriff T-shirt. Pretty sexy, except for the little black socks she had on but I was finding a way to look past them.

When Jane was done she came and sat down next to me in our usual configuration of sitting sideways on the couch so we could face each other. I was aroused from watching her, which made it easy to begin my reframe to get my brain in the correct place to hear her story.

The share was a hookup that started with a massage. Jane loved massages and when I was out of town and unable to provide, she would generally get an in-house massage through one of the city's many massage services. On this particular afternoon, the masseur that came over was a good-looking Belorussian.

She wasn't particularly attracted to him but as the massage started, she noticed it was taking on a very different feel from what she was used to. He was going painstakingly slow as he worked her legs, and as he continued up her thighs, he went far higher than what might be considered acceptable. Still, it wasn't quite far enough to be outright sexual touching. Then he seemed to linger way longer then was needed while up there, and then on her butt as well. Apparently, he had a skilled touch and Jane was beginning to slowly get aroused by the way he was teasing the hell out of her. She had no idea if it was on purpose or not and didn't know what to do. It was kinda fun hearing her frustrated like that and I was getting into it.

My eyes were devouring this woman next to me, sitting in her thong, her long, shapely legs front and center in my field of vision. Maybe she felt it too, sitting there half-naked, because something in how she was telling her story came off like an erotic reading. My imagination took this a step further and I pretended it *was* a private erotic reading. Given to me by some hot underwear model, having nothing to do with Jane. Reframing at a whole new level. Jane continued.

As he moved to work on her upper body, again he came dangerously close to her nipples, continuing to push the edge of what could be considered acceptable. Before he finished though, the timer went off for the end of the ninety-minute massage. He quickly said not to worry about it. He knew he had gotten carried away with her legs so it was on him to continue since she had signed up for a full-body massage. There would be no extra charge for the time.

At this point, Jane described being so aroused that she was aware of a puddle developing between her legs on the massage table. She had no idea if he had noticed.

After two hours and fifteen minutes he finished, and she wondered if he was going to make a move, as the entire thing had been incredibly erotic. But he just left the room to wash his hands while she was supposed to get dressed. She decided to put only her robe on, and when he came back in, she offered to pay him for the extra time, but he refused. Not to be deterred from what she wanted at this point, she asked if she could give him a hug, which he accepted.

She put her arms around him, pressed her body into his, and could easily feel his half-hard cock through his sweatpants. Unable to hold back any longer she dropped to her knees and started sucking his cock to get him fully hard before bending over the massage table pausing only to hand him a condom from the pocket of her robe. You gotta hand it to her, the woman was always prepared.

While Jane was describing all this, I relaxed in a way I had not previously and I'm sure my eyes lit up as they locked on hers. Jane responded to my engagement, put a hand on my leg, and started rubbing me, slowing inching up to my belt as she continued with the story. When she unzipped my pants, my body instantly reacted. Jane leaned forward so that she could whisper in my ear while her hand began stroking my now very hard cock. Her story finished with quite the happy ending for me.

Had I accidentally found the secret? That I could reframe Jane as a completely different person, eliminating the fear and jealousy? And then she would respond to the attention I was giving her by making the moment intimate with her touch, bringing us together physically and emotionally? Or is it that you can pretty much say anything to me while you're stroking my cock and I'll sit there and listen. Jury is still out on that one.

It ended up being a wonderful evening, with Jane really focusing on me and my enjoyment while recounting her story. I felt like something had broken through that night. The confidence I gained from that evening, and how I got through it, made me sort of look forward to sharing nights. I was off to the races.

At the time, I assumed that the breakthrough meant I had fully transcended the insecurities lurking in my psyche. But all I had really done was find a way to bypass the minefield of emotional responses to her behavior. My god, I was naive. I don't fault myself for this though—I had achieved what felt like a major accomplishment, and it was. I was able to listen to things that were incredibly difficult for me, and as a result, we were growing closer.

I had needed to find a way to continue without constantly being distracted by punches to the face, and that's what I did. So if I got a little cocky, thinking that I had the whole thing figured out and had grown in the ways I wanted, well, it certainly wasn't the first time in my life that I had made that mistake. It felt like I was seeking the risk rather than the reward, and it had resulted in the growth I was looking for. Nothing could stop me. I had my strategies in place. Jane and I were making it work, and the results were stellar.

> *Excerpt from Jane's blog:*
> The rules for what I am supposed to tell my husband have changed somewhat over the years. In the beginning, he didn't want to know. It was technically a "don't ask, don't tell" policy. Then, as he got more secure in our relationship, he started letting me share more, usually the basics: who and when, but not all the details. He's now at a point where he wants to know everything, but only:
>
> 1) After it has happened. He says that knowing about it ahead of time makes him create all sorts of stories in his mind about what's going to happen—and that uncertainty is anxiety-provoking and distressing. Once it's happened,

there are no uncertainties. The reality is always less scary than the imagination.

2) Every sexcapade of mine needs some processing on his part. And he's not always in the right mental state to put in that kind of effort. So he wants to be confronted with that information only when he's ready.

And that's currently my biggest challenge—to wait for that moment when I'm supposed to tell him about it. I always want to share a great experience with him immediately, and often forget to wait. But I keep trying. And he is slowly getting used to it.

As he says, "I always expect that you are fucking someone else every night I'm out of town."

Chapter 9
Fight Club

Jane's sex positivity activism was beginning to make her something of a social media personality and at the end of the year she did a wrap-up post of her highlights. In it she mentioned that she was falling in love. As I read that line, I stopped and thought, "Yep, she's right. We are." On an approach to some outdoor adventure with my climbing partner I said to him, "I think my wife is falling in love with me." He just stopped, looked at me, and said, "Do you understand how strange a sentence that is?"

I know that falling in love was surprising to Jane, and myself, to a degree, although I had hoped we would end up there. Oddly, I don't think either of us really expected the relationship to last. Who knows, maybe our lack of expectations took the pressure off, and we just were able to be ourselves.

Initially, I went after Jane for the crazy sex life, but it ended up being a match like no other I'd ever had. Never had I felt so free to be just who I am. Never had I felt so honest with myself. Despite the challenges, the Faustian bargain was proving to be less of a deal with the devil and more a hell-raising love story.

Some folks we knew invited us to go to Burning Man with them. We continued going on outdoor adventures out west. We were living it up in the city that was our playground. I was feeling good that I had successfully pulled out of the relationship nosedive, and the plane was now gaining altitude. I was navigating the emotional minefields with more of a calculating approach. I had found a way to dodge the worst parts of the jealousy and continue getting closer to Jane. Confidence was high, and (to continue to mix metaphors) I thought nothing could derail me now.

***

After Jane moved to New York, her blending of the city's party and academic scenes continued to develop. Jane had a partner in crime, Sophie, who had also recently gotten a PhD in psychology and loved to hit the nightlife social scene in the same way that Jane did. On more than one occasion I had to leave a party without Jane because she and Sophie wanted to stay up all night together. They were inseparable and quite the duo visually. Sophie was soft and bubbly and combined a slight, unassuming frame with a bohemian look, compared to Jane's broader build, dominant personality, and sexually suggestive style.

Luckily for me, Sophie was far more sexually reserved so they didn't have the type of friendship that would have amplified Jane's already-wild sexual lifestyle.

When Sophie was between houses, she came to stay with us for a few weeks. We had an extra bedroom, and we also liked having company. It was lovely having her around, and the three of us had a great time together. But Sophie had not been feeling well. Her appetite was almost nonexistent, so while she was staying with us, she decided to go get checked out.

Jane and I were standing in the kitchen when she called to let us know they had checked her into the hospital and were keeping her overnight for tests. In the next few days we found out it was advanced stomach cancer. Sophie was given six months to live.

After hanging up the phone, Jane came over and just hugged me. This was the first time in her adult life she had been coming up against mortality of someone close to her. We stood there in the kitchen embracing each other, trying our best to keep the rest of the world out. Jane, in general, was not an emotional person, as she had learned early on that if you showed weakness, such as emotions, someone would exploit it at worst, ignore it at best. So when the Eastern European tiger showed her soft underbelly, and the tender and fragile child came to the surface, all I wanted to do was protect her.

It was heartbreaking, but Jane set to the task of being the support person as best she could for Sophie. I was so impressed with Jane, and trying to see a silver lining, I wondered if maybe this was the event that might unlock the empathy and softer side in her, much the same way Tommy's death had unlocked something in me.

They were getting so close during this period; it was beautiful and painful all at the same time. There were all kinds of necessary arrangements to be made and plans about how to spend the remaining days. Having already lost several close friends, I understood what Jane was going through and I tried to support her while she was overwhelmed with Sophie.

If I only had six months to live, what would I be willing to do? The friends that I've lost went quickly, without any opportunity to fill in the missing pieces of their experience.

When Tommy died, some people said that it was probably for the best, as he would have been paralyzed from the chest down if he had lived. But I always pushed back on that. Tommy would have found a way to live his crazy life just the same as he did when he had use of his legs. Hell, I wish he had been given six months to live, even paralyzed. We could have killed it. BASE jumps in a wheelchair; first paralyzed man to do an Alleycat race in NYC traffic on a hand-cranked bike. As his inevitable end drew near, maybe we'd all do one last skydive together—except he wouldn't pull the rip cord, the last rush of his life being the ground rush of the Earth coming to meet him on his terms.

I do wish I'd had that perspective when Jane told me about one of Sophie's dying requests. She had asked Jane to set up a sex night for them, with two men, so she could get double penetrated. Jane also told me I was not invited to be part of it. I knew this was because Sophie and I didn't have any sexual attraction to each other, and not because anyone was trying to hurt me, but still, it stung badly.

I went to a dark place about the event but kept these feelings to myself for obvious reasons. I'd put structures in place to avoid just this sort of situation, one that was so difficult for me—knowing about a hookup of Jane's before it happened. And with this specific hookup, I had plenty of time to make all kinds of assumptions about the event itself, about how emotional and intimate it was going to be. There was no doubt in my mind it would be an intense bonding experience between the men, Jane, and Sophie. How could it not? Soon Sophie would be gone, and it would just be Jane and these two men that had this connection that I wasn't a part of. Like embers that had been smoldering belowground all along, my jealousy flared up into a blazing fire. At the same time, wondering how I could be so shallow was tearing me to pieces. How could I be more concerned with my own emotional safety than with Sophie's life? I didn't know how to process what I was feeling. I was in over my head.

Sophie and Jane started searching the hookup apps and going out to bars to try and land the right male duo for the event. I stewed, not knowing how to deal with it, and with no way to pull the plug other than walking away from Jane. The emotions were intense and overwhelming. It took a few weeks, but they finally found their guys, and a night was set.

I went out west and had no choice but manage to the best of my ability. The night of the event itself, I distracted myself by having dinner with friends and then a movie. On my way to bed I figured I would text Jane, since with the time difference it would probably be all over by then. I got no answer, nor did I wake up the next morning to a text or a missed call. I felt thrown away. I felt like I was losing Jane. I had total attitude failure, and collapse of my mindset. I wanted to send angry texts and voicemails, which would have been about the worst possible thing I could have done, although it most certainly would have made me feel better in the moment. No reframe was working and I was seriously failing at smoking my proverbial cigarette.

I went into full-on blame mode, totally ignoring any part of the reaction that was rooted in "my own shit." The emotional pressure had been building up, and now it was looking for a way out without my ego having to take the hit. *Bam!* Suddenly, there I was again, feeling like the geeky redheaded kid on the playground, left out and alone. Fueled by my oldest childhood fears, my immature self-preservation mechanism was wanting to lash out at her.

I couldn't work; I had no focus. I was so broken I didn't even have the energy to get in the truck and go into the mountains. My imagination was in overdrive, creating the story that Jane must have had a spectacular evening, had met someone who was better equipped for her lifestyle, and was now moving on. My worst fears were proving true. I was angry, depressed, shocked, confused, but yet . . . there was a part of my brain that was telling me I was overreacting. A little voice saying, "You don't really know what happened. All you know is at the moment you are powerless to change anything about the situation, and until Jane calls, you are in that powerless place. That's the real thing that's destroying you."

Whatever was going on, I was at a loss. It was late morning and I left my house to wander around the small downtown in search of some breakfast. Every object in view seemed strange, almost surreal, lawn, house, plants, street. The world felt raw.

After eating breakfast, like a zombie I ambled over to a coffee shop to try to "work" but I was just trying to be around people. The town is so small that inevitably if you're sitting in one of the shops, a friend will come in and sit down with you for a moment. Because I grew up in NYC, this was something that was so unique and lovely to me. To always be able to see someone you know. Just by leaving the house, I was able to have that random connection that could make everything appear okay.

"Hey, how are you?"

"Fine, good, just working away, you know."

"How's Jane doing?"

"Oh good, trying to get her latest research paper finished, normal stuff."

A master class in acting that I assume we all go through at points in our life. When the confusion of living a human existence smacks up against the realities of our ego and privacy. Feign normalcy and maybe everything will be normal for a few minutes. But when my brain is this distracted, I can barely focus on what the other person is saying. Just nod and smile and try to pay attention enough to ask a question about whatever the topic is. The attempt at conversation with another person made me realize just how spun up I was.

I looked around the coffee shop at the other people, at the chairs, the tables, the baristas. Everything was so regular life, totally opposite to the fire that was raging in my head. I spent most of the day in a very dark place, with an inner conversation running nonstop in my head. It got exhausting, and when Jane still hadn't called by the afternoon, I was sunk, beaten. I got the phone out and started to call her several times to let my anger rage, to tell her how she had no hope in life if she didn't understand the value of what we had. So angry that I had made a grand effort at this relationship only to have it be thrown away in an instant. But again . . . the little voice was always there to prevent me from completing the call.

"You just don't know what's going on. Let go of the need for control and just sink into the emotion. You're going to feel crappy till Jane calls. You can wait."

Besides, I knew that calling to yell at her at that moment versus waiting until she inevitably called was just about trying to control the situation, trying to feel like I was the strong, powerful one driving the narrative. If you want to be strong, Adam, chill the fuck out, and go about your life till Jane calls. Exist in that gray area of not knowing and be at peace with it until the time is right to not be peaceful.

At about 6 p.m. the phone rang. It was Jane. I stared at her name on the phone screen and just held onto that moment of still not knowing if my world was about to be completely upended. Feigning total chillness, I answered and said hello in a very nonemotional way, betraying neither happiness nor anger, but trying to suggest that I was intrigued, which would allow me to go either direction once I had a read on what had happened.

The moment I heard Jane's voice, I could tell how elated she was. Her energy was on fire and my body was absorbing it through the phone. I was put off balance by that, and by her repeatedly saying how much she loved me, but it was certainly better than the outcome I had been imagining. Derailed from my anger and my plan of laying into her, I probed for more info. She launched into an excited description of the evening, which was, she exclaimed, the most amazing time. The four of them spent nearly twenty-four hours having sex and it had been the perfect thing for Sophie, who, as I knew, didn't have a lot of perfect things left. All in all, it had been a wonderful experience for the two of them to share. I sat there in a state of shock, deeply affected by the humanity of the event. A dying woman's wish to experience something that only Jane could so easily navigate to fruition for her.

Sharing the details on the phone was breaking our format of waiting till I was back home, but I had known about the event already and had asked. In hearing about the night, in seeing the beauty in the event, and in feeling how happy Jane was that she had been able to provide this experience for her friend, I just listened, so confused about everything *I* was feeling.

Jane and I spent a long time on the phone together just being connected with each other—her breaking down to me about Sophie, the two of us talking about anything, everything, and nothing. We ended the two-hour call and I just sat there with myself. At some level I still felt like a broken man, but broken in such a different way than I had felt throughout the day. Why had I had such an emotional collapse before I knew anything? Why had I assumed the worst possible outcome for me? I had been doing so well lately at this extreme non-monogamy thing, getting through the tough emotions with my sharing protocols and reframing strategies, that it was hard to take what felt like many steps backward. I didn't want to admit that maybe I hadn't really grown as much as I thought I had.

Jealousy had taken hold of me and sent my imagination into overdrive just when the stakes were high. A bad decision made in the heat of the moment that morning might not have cost me my life, as it so easily could on a mountain, but it could have cost me the relationship and the life I loved. I felt lucky that I hadn't picked up the phone and launched into a nasty diatribe at Jane or to her voicemail. The difference between success and failure had been a razor thin line of self-control.

If I wanted to be with Jane long-term, I was going to have to start figuring out how to combat the jealousy, not just dodge it. I'd been dodging it with the "relationship rule" that I would go out west so she could have her hookups without me. I'd been dodging it by strategically avoiding social media when I knew there would be things I didn't want to see. I'd been dodging it with reframing techniques that lessened the emotional impact when she was sharing her experiences with me. All this dodging made sense. It got me to a place where I wasn't in a constant state of agitation and could enjoy what was otherwise a very rewarding relationship.

It seemed to have gotten me this far, but it was going to take me no further. I thought I had left the major minefields behind, but it was apparent from this event that they were still there, and still dangerous. I'd just found routes that bypassed them. I needed to dig deep into my emotional response to Jane's foursome with Sophie and truly understand what I was feeling and why. I had paid a steep price for these emotions, so I figured I probably shouldn't waste the opportunity while my soul was bared.

Let's Go to the Videotape

I knew jealousy was a normal emotion, so it's not like I thought something was wrong with me for feeling it. But I wanted to truly understand it, because it didn't seem to be the whole story for me. This situation in particular felt like a complete failure of self-confidence, especially since it seemed that Jane was even more in love with me after it, the exact opposite of what my brain had been telling me.

What were the thoughts that I could associate with this situation and how I had felt while it was going on? Sitting in my place, alone, somewhat in the dark, as the sun had set without my turning on more lights, the engineer in me got out a notebook and started writing down my thoughts. I felt disrespected at the lack of communication, which was totally valid, but I also felt worthless, powerless, and unseen. Admitting these last three emotions was hard. I stared at those three words.

Worthless

Powerless

Unseen

"How is this possible? I'm one of the toughest men I know. I've done things in situations that would leave most guys frozen with fear. I've stared death in the face over and over again and performed flawlessly when I've had seconds to live if I didn't. This is fucking BULLSHIT!"

It felt like I considered myself a heavyweight champion and then one nice right hook had put me down on the mat. If felt like all this confidence and toughness was just an act, and in reality, I had just never been hit correctly. One solid punch landed and down I went. I wrote "Single Punch Knockout" on my pad, but as I looked at the words, it didn't feel right. The more I thought about it, to stay with the boxing metaphor, first came a good jab, followed by a strong uppercut, which allowed the right hook to do its damage. Fucking textbook knockout combination. I needed to go back to the film and watch it in slow motion to see how it had happened. See the setup, see the obvious signs I was missing, and how my opponent got inside on me so easily.

First there was the jab to the face that landed and knocked me off-balance: a hookup in the future that I was aware of, which was something I had been struggling with. When one of Jane's hookups was in the past, and I was hearing about it at story time, the guys she had hooked up with were gone, and I was still there with Jane. But if I knew about the hookup beforehand, my impostor syndrome would kick in and had plenty of time to create all kinds of stories about what would happen, how being with another guy would expose me for the impostor I really was. Not knowing the outcome and being powerless as it approached were too much for me.

Another important factor, I realized, was being the sexual neophyte in the relationship, something I had never experienced as an adult. I wrote down, "Am I a sexual novice?" Embarrassingly, I had to admit there was a part of me that always felt I had something to prove with Jane.

It had always been there, something in my head trying to tell me that I wasn't good enough, and that any success or indication of ability was a fluke. It had been a battle my entire life, and while I exuded a huge amount of confidence in most situations, there had always been that voice telling me it was just an act, that I wasn't as good as I presented. I wrote down the words "impostor syndrome."

Had I been in therapy at the time, which probably would have been a good idea, I'm sure it would have been front and center that this was not a healthy position to constantly be in.

But that was just the jab to the face. After that had set me off-balance, the hard uppercut to the chin did a bit of damage. I was specifically excluded from the event. I wrote the word "excluded." Intellectually, I knew this was because Sophie and I had no sexual attraction to each other, but wow, did that take me back to the playground. It was literally the same feeling as I remember having when I was told I couldn't play whatever game the other kids were playing. Was this because I wasn't cool enough, too much of the geeky ginger?

Waiting for Jane to call, wandering around town, overcome by negative emotions, that was exactly how I felt when I was a 13-year-old kid on some Saturday afternoon hanging out by myself, feeling like I had no friends because I wasn't invited to be part of something that was going on. Of course, this was before cell phones and email so in reality it might have been just a question of logistics, or there might have actually been nothing going on. It was irrelevant. I was feeling young, alone, and powerless. I was excluded and felt that nobody liked me. I couldn't believe it. "Here I am in my forties, and my emotions are operating off of perceived things that happened to me thirty years ago." Regardless of how ridiculous it was, it was as real and powerful as it had been when I was 13. I wrote, "I'm not fucking 13 anymore," and then angrily underlined it three times.

That uppercut after the jab had stung and rung my bell, setting me up for the knockout punch, the right hook of Jane not calling to check in. I wrote down, "Jane didn't call." That was the only real punch that I should have expected to land, and in all fairness to me, her behavior was bullshit. Jane should have checked in by the morning. I mean who the fuck has a foursome with their dying friend and two rando guys, and then doesn't call their husband to check in at some point? Right? I'm sure we've all gone through this, so you know what I'm talking about. But Jane's failure required a discussion and should not have had the impact of a relationship-ending event, which is what it felt like to me at the time. In hindsight, it was a discussion that I should have had with her, but I was too overcome with the other emotional challenges to recognize that at the time.

The pressure had been building inside me from the moment I first heard about Sophie's plan, and I was now starting to see that

I had been primed into an agitated state by my personal issues, unaware of the control they had on me. When Jane didn't call that evening or the next morning, the pressure blew, and I exploded. If I hadn't been in that heightened state, I probably would have told her that her behavior was disrespectful. That would have been the evolved response.

Having reviewed the film of how I got knocked out, I put the pen down and got to work. I still had two weeks on my own out west before heading home so it was a good time to start sinking into Socrates and the whole examined life thing.

Leaving the missed phone call out of it, since that was on her, I moved on to the jealousy, which was based on things that had nothing to do with Jane, other than insofar as her behavior exposed them. That took me back to the uppercut that did so much damage, being excluded. The playground stuff was interesting to me. Was it appropriate that I was still holding onto this childhood image as the lens I saw everything through, as an overarching narrative of my entire life? Did the image have any relation to reality, then or now?

I honestly had no idea how often things like that truly had happened to me back then. I was certainly teased about being a ginger on occasion, and I was excluded from things now and again, as all kids probably were. But in taking a deep look at my life, excluded was the last thing in the world that was happening to me. I had an engaged, vibrant, and diverse set of friends. I'd had no lack of love and physical intimacy with amazing women. I felt that I'd lived several lifetimes already and people who I deeply respected seemed to be very interested in spending time with me. This idea of being the redheaded geek on the playground that nobody wants to play with was, when I looked at the facts, totally false. But there it was, still taking me down and taking me down hard.

I was beginning to have some understanding about the stinging uppercut I had taken to the chin. It was based on irrational fears that were in direct conflict with the reality of my life.

Then I turned my attention to the initial jab to the face. My diagnosis was that it caught me in the raw, weak spot of my impostor syndrome. Once again, there was no data to suggest that I was actually an impostor. Professionally, I had accomplished a lot after taking huge risks, and many talented people had willingly joined me on my projects and loved getting involved. Yet this impostor syndrome was constantly there and it was a biggie. It had been a dominating, negative force on my emotions for as long as I could remember. Where did that come from?

My earliest memories of it were from grade school. I know this is going to sound crazy, but I think my friends were too smart. There was a small group of us that got together in first grade, when we had all been admitted to the same gifted-and-talented program. We continued together till we graduated high school and are still close to this day. And while I don't consider myself stupid by any stretch of the imagination, this group seemed to have brainpower at an uncommon level, excluding myself, of course. Because I had never been superstrong academically, I felt like I was the odd one out, and I was always trying to hide what I perceived as my intellectual failings from them. I always felt that it had been a mistake that I had been included in the program, so I thought I had to keep faking it to fit in.

Now in all fairness to me, this group did have a very strange mix of the biggest brains you could meet. Three of them are at the top of the world in their chosen academic fields, and the others are intellectual powerhouses in their own right. True geniuses. It was as if I had grown up with several Michael Jordans, and concluded that I sucked at basketball (which I kinda do, but that's beside the point).

Moving into my twenties, and still haunted by this childhood fear, I was dominated by the drive to prove myself to others. To women, I was trying to prove I was desirable, to men I was trying to prove I was a worthy opponent, one who commanded respect and was tough as nails in the face of danger. That was at the peak of my trophy-bagging days, when trophies were the measuring stick I used to gauge where I was on the org chart with the other guys.

In my late twenties I worked hard to get away from the idea that each competition was a life-or-death battle to prove I wasn't an impostor. I realized that proving myself to other people was taking away from my ability to just be in the moment and enjoy the activity at hand. I also recognized that no matter how many women I slept with, or how many times I stared death in the face, I'd never win, the fight would never be over. It was a dumb fight.

Now, for the first time in my life, I was being overwhelmed by jealousy, but jealousy, from what I can tell, is a complex emotion that can have different origins, depending on the person. The powerful engine for the jealousy I was feeling was fear that I was going to be exposed as an impostor.

Wow. Was I still so influenced by my early experiences of feeling that I wasn't good enough to be picked to be part of the game that even after Jane and I had picked each other, I was continually in a frantic state, trying to make sure nothing happened that would reveal I shouldn't have been picked in the first place? No wonder that jab to the face of knowing about a future hookup of Jane's had knocked me off balance so badly.

When Jane and I first started spending more time together, I had the normal concerns that she would meet somebody else, or that one of her hookups would morph into something more, but I was able to put those feelings aside back then. They were just the regular machinations of dating. Was it just that I was more invested now? If that was true, then it should reason that as we were getting more emotionally involved with each other, she was becoming more invested as well, and that the likelihood of her leaving me was far less. Or perhaps the fact that we were more emotionally involved was precisely what was scaring me. It meant the "fall" would hurt a lot more if that happened.

But we had been involved for almost four years now, living together for the last two, and logic dictated that if I truly were an impostor, especially in the sexual realm, it most certainly would have been exposed by that point. I'd been with a good number of women over the years, and had confidence in my sexual abilities, but it was different with Jane. With her I felt, comparatively speaking, inexperienced. And I had never had a relationship in which my girlfriend was routinely sleeping with other men. These two realities were rocket fuel for my impostor syndrome. And yet, the reality was, we'd been growing closer for the entire time we'd been together. I'm the only man Jane has ever stayed with for that long, and sex is quite important to her so I must be doing something right. Right? Once again, I needed to pay attention to the facts of my life, and not listen to the voices in my head.

> *Excerpt from Jane's blog:*
> Last week, I overheard my husband chatting with a guy friend who's been dating a younger girl for the past few months.
>
> **ADAM:** So, how's it going with your new girlfriend?
>
> **FRIEND:** Oh, it's awesome. She's only slept with two people. She thinks I'm really great in bed.
>
> **ADAM:** Yeah, my wife thinks I'm pretty good too. She's slept with six hundred people. I trust her opinion on this subject.
>
> **FRIEND:** Hmm, good point.

Well wasn't this just perfect. I had figured out that I wasn't an impostor. Congratulations, Adam. But now I was feeling like a fucking idiot. Of course, this was easy enough for me to reason out during my thought experiment, but it wasn't so easy in the heat of the moment. My psychological baggage was overriding the facts, and rational thought was not what my brain seemed to naturally swing toward when my qualifications were the subject. Instead, my brain created a powerful negative outcome fantasy. Then it would live in it and feel the emotions around it.

But a fantasy is just that, a fantasy. If I could have looked into the future and seen how powerful the experience would be for Jane, and how it would actually bring Jane closer to me, how would my experience have been different? The story I had created was so far away from what actually transpired, and I was blown away by how my imagination had controlled me.

I thought about how happy it had made Jane to be able to provide this experience for Sophie. I thought about how happy she was to talk to me afterward. I thought about how this whole experience had added to her own experience-hunting life and I loved her for that. The simple truth was that my life was going to improve because Jane was in a better place. Here I was on this emotional free solo, getting exactly what I had been going after with Jane—one hell of a wild ride.

Beaten and broken, lying on the canvas, I was finally able to see how the dark forces of my brain were controlling me. They were selling me this idea of myself, this fantasy—and for the first time in my life I could *feel* that it wasn't real. This feeling was momentous. It's one thing to intellectually understand something, but it's another thing to really know it in your heart, to feel it.

As I looked at the arc of my relationship with Jane and beyond, I could see how my imagination had been dictating the narrative for most of my life, and I had been completely unaware of it.

The more I looked, the more I was getting a sense of everything I had accomplished, and how the voices were holding me back from feeling what a beautiful and wonderful person I was, from feeling pride in how I had always pushed myself to go to the uncomfortable places in my head. I made a commitment that those fantasies would never have a devastating effect on me anymore.

When the irrational fears started bubbling to the surface, I wouldn't try to reframe them. I had to attack the root of the problem by recognizing them for what they were, a false narrative. The hard part was that the emotions these false narratives invoke are real and powerful, so it was going to be imperative for me stay in the concrete reality of what my life really was. I needed to start keeping all this data about myself in the forefront of my consciousness. That way, in tough moments, I could remember who I was and who I wasn't.

From my years of climbing, I knew that the mental battle to stay calm and focused was purely an internal one—and it was the same thing here. When I lifted the mask off my opponent, the one who landed the crushing blows, it wasn't Jane, or Sophie, or the other guys I was looking at, it was me. There I was, staring right into my own eyes and face. I had been fighting myself the entire time, and I was the toughest opponent I had ever encountered. Brutal, unrelenting, no mercy. There was no Tyler Durden.

My epiphany allowed me to start thinking about the experience more rationally, and I had the awareness to recognize the one person I was forgetting about. Sophie, who had but a few months to live. I wondered how she had woken up the next morning after the wild twenty-four hours she'd had. What had she thought about the experience? Was it everything she had hoped it would be? Did she feel more prepared for the end of her life? What was she thinking?

Thinking about her and that night now, years after her death, brings back powerful emotions. In the remaining time she had, that night was one of the things that she had chosen to make sure happened. Luckily for her, Jane was exactly the best friend she needed for it. Death isn't something any of us can escape, and if she in that moment, in that event, found some peace or satisfaction, I feel glad that I was able to control myself enough to not blow the whole thing up. It's a thin prize, but I'll take it.

The next time I saw Sophie was the last time I saw her alive. I was speaking with someone who basically knew the date of their own death, and it was right around the corner.

At the memorial service, Jane was asked to say a few words. She spent quite a bit of time on what she was going to say, but shortly after beginning she abandoned her prepared eulogy and gave an off-the-cuff emotional, bright, happy, tear-filled account of how wonderful Sophie had been to her and what a light she was. Telling funny stories about them together that really highlighted the humanness of celebrating a life. Standing in the back of the room, I was so moved by her words and her ability to show how much Sophie had meant to her.

When Jane finished and came back to me, she asked if she had blown it by being so haphazard and not reading what she had written. I told her it was perfect and gave her a big hug. Sometimes life stops you for a moment and shows you what's really important. Sophie's death provided that moment for Jane and me.

With this perspective inspiring me, during my subsequent trips out west, I continued working my way through the epiphanies I'd had. Then when I was back east, I would put my newfound awareness into practice. Little by little, I was sorting it out. I could feel that something significant was shifting within me. I recognized how much I had been shooting myself in the foot over and over again. And just recognizing that was usually enough to remind me before I pulled the trigger yet again—it's just a false narrative. I'd review the data of my life. It *was* just a false narrative. My finger would ease off the trigger.

As I began sinking into my new awareness, I noticed my life with Jane was becoming significantly more enjoyable. My ability to feel the depth of our connection, to feel how valuable I was to the relationship, dramatically reduced the impact of her sexual exploits. It was as if I had been seeing a monster under the bed for years and when I finally got out a flashlight and looked at it, it was just a pile of dirty clothes.

Am I a Fucking Adult Now?

My life was transforming. I was significantly more relaxed about the things in Jane's life that had been so hard for me to absorb. Share time was starting to become fun and funny. A lightness was emerging when we would talk about hookups. I kept the data points I needed in the forefront of my consciousness so when the negative outcome fantasies came up, I could see right through them and lovingly laugh at myself. As a result, I found that I was taking myself less seriously and seeing the absurdity of my life in ways I hadn't before. I mean sheesh, really? I'm married to someone who's fucking around seventy-five guys a year. If you can't find the absurdity in that . . .

With the monster exposed for what it was—just my imagination—I began to get more curious about the entire endeavor, about the reality of the fact that other men in Jane's life were there. In this new frame of mind, other men and the reactions they caused started to become interesting to me. I'd set aside sexual competition as juvenile long ago, but now that I didn't feel driven to overcompensate for my impostor syndrome, I began to see competition in a new light.

I asked myself, "What if someone is better than me at sex?" I mean, is it reasonable to think I am the be-all and end-all of sex for Jane? This brought me back to the sex party where I had walked in on her with three guys. Right before that, I had been observing a cunnilingus competition between the husband of the woman and another man. Here was a husband sharing his wife with this guy, something Jane and I had certainly done, but this was under the format of a competition. Or I should say, under the explicit format of a competition. I was starting to see that I had always been in competition with the other men in Jane's life, even when we were all "working together" as a threesome.

I reasoned that as far as the woman at that party was concerned, competition was definitely good for the consumer. I started laughing. It was a goofy way to look at it, but I continued down this line of thinking. I was the corporation, Jane was the consumer, and sex was the product. In a traditional relationship, I would have a monopoly: the consumer isn't allowed to get the product from anyone else.

But what happens to quality when there is no competition? There is no incentive to improve the product, so the corporation gets lazy. The desire to perform at your peak sexually seems to diminish as the years go by. I had witnessed this dynamic in the long-term relationships around me and I always found it depressing.

I thought about my own dating experiences over my adult life. Things are so charged when I am trying to earn the affection of a potential girlfriend and I'm always trying to be and look my best. I know there is competition, so I would rise to the challenge and show up in every respect.

Given how Jane and I lived, I certainly couldn't take my relationship for granted. I knew there was a ton of competition out there, but frequently I had been letting myself be intimidated by it.

As a competitive athlete for most of my life, I loved competition. It pushed me to be better at things so I could compete at a higher level, which was always very satisfying. It's what drove me to the weight room to gain thirty pounds so I could play ice hockey at the collegiate level. It's what drove me to train fifteen hours a week on my bike for several years so I could have a decent amateur racing career. After all, if I played a sport without any competition, how good would I get? Would I even feel motivated to improve my game? If I only played against people who were worse than I was, would I even feel the need to improve?

The entire non-monogamy thing began to appear in a whole new light for me. With a solid partner, one who I knew respected and cared for me, non-monogamy had the potential to be the kind of healthy competition I had always craved, the kind that drove me to be the best I could be. I also recognized that I abhor a steady-state existence, and non-monogamy was the antithesis of that. A healthy level of competition provided a nice framework to motivate me to show up as an actively participating partner in this relationship. I began leaning into non-monogamy in a healthy way for the first time since Jane and I got together. Finally, I was starting to feel that I was growing in the ways I'd been hoping to and that my struggles were beginning to pay major dividends.

A few months later, the topic of non-monogamy came up at a dinner party, as it usually does when Jane and I are in mixed company and people are curious about our lifestyle. I took the opportunity to float my philosophy of competition being good for the consumer, and that it drove me to be a better partner. Jane looked at me with a smile and said she had never heard me say that before, but she really liked it.

***

I hadn't known it, but when I met Jane, I *was* still fragile around sex and relationships for reasons that had nothing to do with sex or relationships—and I had gone after a partner who, just by being the person she was, took me right back into the middle of my very own emotional minefield.

It was sobering to realize how naive and overconfident I had been going in, but also reassuring that I was still the experience hunter running toward the burning building. My epiphany in the aftermath of the Sophie foursome didn't change my life overnight, but it started me down the right path. I was seeing myself and the negative thoughts I had about myself more clearly. Yes, things were still difficult, and reaching a guru state of non-monogamy was still a lofty and distant goal, but there I was, successfully sinking into myself, into Jane, into healthy competition, and into this crazy relationship. I was feeling pretty fucking good about what I had managed to work through.

ACT III

Chapter 10
Hitting My Stride

Excerpt from Jane's blog:

Last night I orchestrated a threesome with my friend Marilyn and my husband Adam. I know he had been lusting after her for a while as she's kind of his perfect body type, so it was wonderful to see the excitement and pleasure in his eyes as the evening wore on. At one point Adam was fucking her from behind when she started moaning how big his cock was, over and over again.

"It's so big, it's so big . . ."

I was thinking to myself that it's really not that big, when all of a sudden, I accidentally said it out loud.

"It's not *that* big."

The words landed, Adam and Marilyn froze for a long second . . . then burst out laughing.

Oh well.

Things were falling into place nicely. I was getting so relaxed with our lifestyle and feeling confident in a way I hadn't for some time. I even decided to tell my parents about our open marriage. They were getting on in years and I wanted to make sure I didn't have any regrets after they were gone about them not really knowing me. I assumed they were unaware of how Jane and I lived, given that they weren't on social media, and we didn't really run in the same circles.

Sitting in their living room one evening when I was over for dinner, I finally came clean.

"Hey guys, I wanted you to know that Jane and I have been having an open marriage. We're not exclusive sexually."

They looked at each other and then at me and my mom said, "Yeah, we know."

I laughed. "How did you know this?"

"Because we can see what goes on around us. Plus, we have friends who are on social media and, well, they like to gossip about scandalous things."

I had really been stressing about telling them, but it turned out it was no issue at all. They said they didn't understand it, but if it worked for me, they were happy. Feeling comfortable enough to tell them was a big deal for me. It showed me how far I had come in my own acceptance of who I was. I was continuing to do the work on myself, identifying the negative thoughts and acknowledging all the positivity. Over time it became a process that ran quietly in the background, always listening in, but only engaging when needed. The adventure was going smoothly. I honestly felt I like I had nailed the Triple Lindy and stuck the landing.

***

As we continued to get closer, my bond with Jane was like nothing I had ever experienced before, and while Jane had had a deep connection before, back in Europe with Astrid, this was the first time she had ever experienced this level of connection with a man. When we started getting more intimate emotionally, Jane was clear with me that Astrid was the love of her life. For some reason, this didn't threaten me, probably because she was on the other side of the Atlantic and, as far as Jane was concerned, that relationship was over. Also, if Jane decided to be with a woman over me, there really wasn't a lot that I could fault myself on. I'm all male, masculine to the core. If she wanted to be with a woman, well, that was just bad luck for me, and not due to any lack on my part.

When we would go over to Europe to see her family and friends, Jane would always spend a couple nights with Astrid, and I was fine with it, especially given that Jane and I would have some good sex beforehand. I was starting to recognize that as long as I was having a deep emotional *and* physical connection with Jane, there wasn't too much that could set me off anymore.

I really liked Astrid from the moment I met her. She was one of the coolest people I've ever known, and I've known a lot of cool people. She worked for a UN mission while also owning and running a small bar in the town where Jane had grown up. She was a wonderful human being, and we developed a kind of friendship. I mean, we both loved the same woman, so we had that in common.

During our trips, many a night was spent at Astrid's bar, which was a regular venue for performance artists. On any given night there would be at least one performance on the small stage in the corner or out front on the old cobblestone walkway. Jane and I had a blast there, laughing it up with Astrid and all her friends as we drank cocktails in her bar, which was tucked into a stone structure built during the Ottoman Empire.

My life and Jane's were starting to entwine in a way that can only be described as traditional. Our friends were becoming friends; our families were getting to know each other. Her mother and sister would come over for Thanksgiving with my family. And given that Jane had a doctorate in developmental psychology, my friends and family would routinely engage with her about difficulties they were having with their children and their relationships. It was feeling so . . . normal.

We were in tune with each other in so many ways. We had been routinely climbing together for several years now, and one afternoon, quite late in the day for such an adventure, we headed out to Rocky Mountain National Park and climbed the Petit Grepon, a thousand-foot granite tower that was a full five miles from the trailhead. We started so late that the sun was setting as we reached the summit and began rappelling back to our waiting packs at the bottom. We hiked out in the dark with our headlamps. This was a testament to how comfortable I was in the outdoors with Jane, and how good we had gotten as a climbing team. I knew we would be off the rock before darkness hit even though we had started the hike in at 2 p.m. We did the entire thing in a quick seven hours from car to car (well, truck anyway). This woman was exactly who I wanted to be with. She lived life at full speed, ballsy as fuck, and always up for an adventure of any kind.

> *Excerpt from Jane's blog:*
> I've currently found someone who fits each of my relationship criteria to at least an acceptable degree, such that the relationship overall adds to my life significantly more than it detracts from it. Whether that will continue to be the case in the future, I don't know. But the minute I feel that either one of us has changed in a way that the relationship is now more of a burden than an asset, I will leave. And I expect him to do the same if he ever feels that way.

Art, theater, climbing, snowboarding, sex. My world was going amazingly well. Given how appreciative Jane was of the judgment-free life she was able to live with me, she went out of her way to make sure I was getting the benefits of her lifestyle.

With her public persona as a sex educator, it was no surprise that she attracted a lot of sex-positive women to her, and I enjoyed many a threesome with Jane and a female friend of hers. The 16-year-old boy in me was losing his shit. And while we had plenty of women join us in the bedroom, it's worth noting that we had many MFM threesomes too. Most of the time she got double penetrated, which was her thing.

> *Excerpt from Jane's blog:*
> The Fireman made sure to let me know that while he was open-minded and looking forward to exploring various possibilities with Adam and me, he was a "flaming heterosexual" and therefore not interested in playing with Adam. I assured him that Adam was just as heterosexual, and that they were both there for my pleasure only.

Given how public Jane was about our sex life, I began to get feedback that the life I was living was causing some of my friends to contemplate their own relationship choices. I didn't really think anyone was going to change their behavior, but the fact that it started the conversations meant that attitudes were shifting and that was rewarding to me.

The Top Floor, Please

Sex parties became an increasingly larger and larger part or our life, and we were easily going to one a month. There is no shortage of such parties in New York City's underground sex world. If you wanted to, you could go to a different sex party several nights a week.

When we first started going to these parties together, I found out the hard way that complex emotions could come at any moment, and they had the potential to send me into a tailspin. So I asked Jane that we have a standing plan to have breakfast the next morning to "debrief" the night with each other, the same strategy my climbing partner and I used after coming off of big climbs.

Just knowing that I'd have an opportunity to raise any concerns the next day always helped take the edge off of the feeling that I needed to react in the heat of the moment. When I floated this to Jane, she was fine with it, which was a nice surprise. Maybe she was softening a bit? In these debriefs, I held back from revealing the full depth of any emotional turmoil I had gone through. I wasn't ready to open up that much to her for fear of turning her off. But I was starting to feel seen, and my needs acknowledged, which apparently went a long way toward helping me immerse myself in the environment. Plus, the debriefs added a nice bookend to the experience.

On the taxi ride home from those parties we would just sit in peace, usually falling asleep against each other while we shot through the darkness, over the Williamsburg Bridge and back to Brooklyn.

Sitting together the next morning, coffees in hand, we would tell each other our stories from the party. Sharing, laughing, and just being silly with each other. It was great how much Jane was on board with all my structures to help keep me grounded. She understood their effectiveness and how much they helped me get more comfortable with how she wanted to live. Her ability, and willingness, to do so played a large part in our success being together. As long as I was making an effort to be stronger, she was right on board with it. But I can see how over time, always having to show strength and never admit to feeling jealousy or insecurity probably wore me out emotionally.

Eventually, I had an opportunity to share some of what I had learned with a close vanilla male friend from my climbing world. One of my closest female friends from our crazy sex life in NYC accompanied Jane on one of her trips out west to come skiing. While she was staying with us, she wanted to get laid with someone new and asked me if I had any cool guy friends for her to hook up with. I introduced her to one of my climbing buddies, hoping that they could have a fun night or two together while she was in town. Unexpectedly, they ended up totally hitting it off.

When she was getting ready to take him to his first sex party, I gave him one piece of advice: "If something happens at the party that really gets at you, you need to chill out and just let it sit. Save the discussion about it for the next day." Since he was a climber, he understood from experience what I was talking about. We don't start shouting fights halfway up on a wall. We finish the adventure, and then review anything that happened when we are back to safety. As of this writing, they are still going strong, having just bought a house together. It was fun because I saw a bit of our own story in theirs.

The parties we went to regularly were run very well, with lots of "guardian angels" floating around the space to make sure everyone had a safe, good time. It was surprising how easy, fun, and enjoyable these events could be, as we had been to plenty of others that weren't.

The first one we attended together on the top floor of that hotel (where I walked in on Jane with the three men) ended up being our favorite, as it was always just one of the best parties period. It was held about four times a year, and we made sure to be at every one. The quality of the experience, I think, had a lot to do with the individual who threw them. He really believed in the sex-positive lifestyle and wanted to create an environment that made everyone feel comfortable and safe enough to explore however much, or however little, they wanted. He accomplished this in a few ways:

1. Anyone could come to the party, but to be invited you had to be recommended by someone who was already a member. If you recommended someone and they screwed up badly in some way, not only would they be asked to leave but your membership would be revoked as well.

2. Prospective invitees didn't have to send a photo to prove that they were "hot" enough (a common requirement at many such events). He was more interested in getting the right vibe than pure eye candy.

3. While the admission price was high, if you couldn't afford it, you could get a free ticket by either working a two-hour shift during the eight-hour party or being part of the setup or breakdown crew. This made sure that there was a good socioeconomic mix, which always makes for a better time.

4. There were an equal number of single men and single women, to keep things balanced and socially equitable.

5. To give it a sense of occasion, the attendees were asked to dress in fancy cocktail attire. One of the events even started with a string quartet performing in one of the rooms.

It wasn't an orgy. It was a classy party, but outrageous in its own way. Walking around the party, you would see sex of some sort going on in various spots throughout the space. Sometimes in the middle of the main room, which was the dance floor. Frequently in the many bedrooms, or even in one of the small hallways. Bathrooms, though, were no-sex zones, so they'd be available for their primary purpose.

It was a judgment-free place where people could be who they were. There were D/s couples— sometimes the woman was being led around by collar and leash, and sometimes it was the man wearing a bridle, with the bit in his mouth. There were female and male gay couples, which is something I had not seen before: heterosexual and homosexual couples engaging in play right next to each other on a bed.

Being able to show up at parties like these with Jane, who had attained celebrity status in the community, was remarkable. We hooked up with couples and individuals alike, having experiences that I thought only existed in fantasies. As someone who had been an athlete my entire life, and had always taken meticulous care of my body, it felt great to have sexy women of all ages appreciating me purely as an object of their desire. It's quite a thing to have a woman you've never met before come up to you, run her hands over your body, and ask you to fuck her right there.

On one occasion I was lying on my back on a bed making out with Jane and a couple of women took turns sucking my cock and then riding it. I was just a living sex toy to them.

Inevitably, there were some funny moments too. On one occasion, I was fucking Jane from behind while she was sucking some other guy's cock when one of the guardian angels for the party came up to me, put his hand on my shoulder and said, "Hey, you need to put a condom on!"

"Hey yourself," I replied, "this is my wife!"

Everyone nearby laughed.

Then there were some completely mind-numbing nights, like the time I had sex with six different women at a single party, which was a new and interesting experience for me (though something Jane had done with men many times). I felt very much like an animal operating on some biological level. I certainly never set out with a "goal" for the evening, other than to have a good time. It just happened organically. Definitely not the geeky ginger anymore.

It was extreme living at a level I had never contemplated. I now had the knowledge of what that was like, which in itself was something, but being with six women in one night didn't leave me with the kind of euphoria my younger self would have expected. Perhaps I was just getting older, but it was too much all at once to fully enjoy the effects of each of the experiences. I'm glad I got to do it, but as I processed the evening, I realized that I would have much rather had six individual nights spread out over a longer period of time so I could bask in the glow of each one.

After that night, sex parties became more of a social event for me. If there was someone I was interested in hooking up with, I would focus on having that experience in a significant way, and then mingling and enjoying the party for the rest of the night.

As time wore on and my business continued to grow, I had to start leaving the parties before it got too late—we now had a staff of forty-five people—so sleep was becoming much more critical for me. But when I started making these needs known, Jane made it clear that she didn't want to leave with me, which was a bit disappointing. I acquiesced to going home alone, even though I knew how much I wanted her to come home with me. Taking our taxi ride together and crawling into bed with each other was just such a nice way to end the evening. It allowed me to feel connected to her no matter how many men and women she might have had sex with that night.

Soon my leaving without her became the rule rather than the exception. Each time I got home from a party and got into bed alone, I felt that something was beginning to slip. That feeling was only reinforced when occasionally I would wake up and Jane hadn't come home yet. The initial discussions we had on the subject made it abundantly clear that I was going to lose this battle if I chose to fight it, so I didn't. I probably should have made a point of voicing how important this was to me and to the health of our relationship. Going home together might have seemed like a small bonding thing but small bonds can carry a lot of weight, and part of me could feel that. Maybe if I'd been clearer about my needs Jane might have said okay. I mean, I doubt it, and present Jane agrees that she would not have acquiesced, but still, I think it would have been better for me personally if I had. No matter what her response, just having that conversation would have helped me assess how healthy our relationship was. I was still stuck in the mindset of don't be the fragile guy, so home alone I went from that point forward.

Of Levees and Lightning

A couple we knew in New York had completely renovated a historic Victorian home in New Orleans and turned it into an event space where they threw wild sex parties. When they invited us to attend one, we gladly accepted and decided to make a long weekend out of it, to give ourselves a chance to see the city.

When we got down there, we bought a pair of cheap cruiser bikes and spent the daylight hours riding all over town. We spent most of one day in the Lower Ninth Ward, riding and walking around, eating in a local restaurant, seeing the destruction from Katrina all those years ago, meeting the residents, talking to them and hearing their stories about the flood.

At one point we locked the bikes and walked up a set of stairs on the northern levee to the Bayou Bienvenue Wetland Platform. From this vantage point, we could look out over the wetland marshes to the north, while behind us was the Lower Ninth Ward. Many of its residents never returned after the flood so much of it was abandoned and overgrown. An older gentleman with a pair of binoculars was looking out over the marsh. I don't know what it was but there was something about him that was compelling. Maybe it was his age. Maybe it was the casual nature of his clothes. Maybe it was his air of regal authority. We were both drawn to him, and we engaged.

He was an environmentalist and a local historian, practically a living library for the Lower Ninth Ward, where he had lived his whole life. We ended up spending a couple of hours with him.

He told us that when he was a boy you could have walked straight across the marshes on all the cypress trees that grew there. But then the Army Corps of Engineers dug the canal to give shipping easier access to the Mississippi River—and the canal gave brackish water a way to enter the wetlands, effectively killing all the native trees and plants. He went on to say that a few years ago, they shut down the canal for good, and he was out there with his binoculars studying the rehabilitation of the wetlands.

From there, he led us around on a walking tour, pointing out significant spots and showing us how much the area had changed since he was a boy. He also recommended a place for us to grab lunch, and which bar we could go to if we needed to buy drugs. Somehow when Jane and I traveled together, we inevitably had these sort of encounters.

After lunch and some more cruising around the Lower Ninth Ward, we headed back across the city to where the house was, on the higher ground of the more affluent Seventh Ward. It made for quite a contrast. The house itself was striking. Imagine an impressively restored Victorian mansion, done up with all the trimmings of late-nineteenth-century Paris meets *Rocky Horror Picture Show*. And to match the house, a lot of the guests had a goth vibe. That was fine with me. I grew up in late '80s NYC so I was completely comfortable with folks wearing black eyeliner and shadow.

The party had a great mix of people. There were exhibitionists, a few cross-dressers, and some furry action (furries are folks who dress up in animal costumes to have sex with each other). There were some hard-core D/s relationships on display. One woman was in a dog cage, and her Dom was making her suck off *any* guy who put his cock through the cage holes. I will admit I did participate in their relationship. There was also regular vanilla sex among the nonkinky partygoers.

My god, this party was fun. It was artistic, sexy, erotic, adventurous, and mysterious. Jane and I were each on our own adventures throughout the evening but kept running into each other in the various sections of the mansion. We would huddle up and update each other on who we had hooked up with, who we wanted to hook up with, and fun spots in the massive house to go check out. We were in the midst of a perfect drop-and-deploy party experience. At one point in the evening, I was part of a crazy threesome performance in the huge kitchen on the main floor with a large crowd watching. Unfortunately, Jane walked in seconds after the climax of the event as we got a round of applause from the impromptu audience, and missed the whole thing.

The long weekend felt like the epitome of us at our best. We had a wonderful moment as we were waiting for the party to start, sitting together on the roof of the house and watching an amazing electrical storm to the north. Snuggled up next to each other, the smell of the Louisiana air, coffees in hand, silent except for the "ooh" and "aah" sounds we were making with each electrical display seemingly better than the last, lighting up the sky in ways neither of us had ever seen.

And yet, despite having this wonderful weekend in New Orleans together, sitting on the plane heading home, we realized that we hadn't actually had sex with each other. Nothing like a romantic getaway to fuck everyone but your spouse. We laughed at that. In hindsight, I wonder if this was a sign of instability that I had been ignoring.

***

Given my growing confidence, it was inevitable that eventually I was going to push myself too far. This came to fruition when at Jane's request, I decided to push past one of the first guardrails Jane and I had adopted when we started living together. The rule in question was that close male friends of mine were off-limits to her.

I had a friend who, oddly, looked a lot like me, and Jane was very attracted to him. We share the same type of build, and we're almost the exact same age. We frequently wear each other's clothes and often get mistaken for each other. Jane really wanted a threesome with the two of us because it was probably as close as she was going to get to having sex with twins. She also happens to have a thing for fit bald men in their forties. Once again, I was presented with a situation that felt scary to me. But while he and I were friends, he wasn't inner-circle close, so I decided he was a reasonable person to try pushing the limit with.

After a fun evening in his hot tub with a tequila or two, the three of us ended up in his bedroom. He and I were all over Jane and she had a great night, with all kinds of crazy configurations and Jane at the center of it all. The evening finished up, and Jane and I went home feeling that his mind had sorta gotten blown in a good way. The emotional work I had to do aside, the evening was superfun, which was all good. As uneasy as I had been about a vanilla friend having sex with Jane, it didn't seem so bad. I wasn't sure I wanted to do it again though. It was emotional work at some level, and I didn't know if there was enough upside to justify it.

Unbeknownst to us, the experience had put my friend a little out of whack in regard to his friendship with me. Whether it was real or just perceived, things felt tense between us for a while. Then I began to feel like he was avoiding me, and there was a bit of drama in our circle of friends over it, nothing too bad, but it had an impact. Additionally, on Jane's subsequent visits out west, he very obviously now thought Jane was fair game for him without checking in to see if I was okay with it. That hurt, even though I knew it was due to his inexperience with open relationships and not in any way out of malice. This was a big aha moment for me.

I realized that if I'm going to engage at that level with a friend, it was important that the friend in question already be familiar with the world of non-monogamy. For the uninitiated, it seemed it was just too much of a mind fuck.

Still, in the end, it all worked out. We're very close now, inner circle close, which is far closer than we were then—but not because of that night. In fact, we laugh about that threesome with some regularity. But due to that entire experience, I decided that the no-close-friends limit was a good one for me. I had gone too far and decided to come back. The rule stayed in place, not to be broken again.

***

Jane's career continued to pick up steam. A book deal was on the table, and she had met an editor for *Cosmopolitan* who asked her to write an article about what goes on at a high-end sex party in New York City. Jane set to the task, taking a bunch of our experiences from three different sex parties and weaving them into a single story. The only problem was that Jane had been in academia her entire life. She had written many scientific research papers that had been peer-reviewed and published. She had written a textbook during her undergraduate work in Europe that was in current use. But she had never written anything with "color" for the general public other than a blog she was starting to play around with based on her antics in NYC.

When I first read what she had written I laughed at how dry and matter-of-fact it was. She was writing from the perspective of a social scientist, not from the perspective of the everyday woman who would be reading it. We set to work on the article together for a good couple of weeks and when it came out, we were superexcited. It was fun to have done that together.

All in all, things were good.

Excerpt from Adam's journal:

> Jane and I went out on a date with another couple last night, hopefully to have a fun night of group sex. That didn't happen but we did have a nice evening chatting with them over drinks. Since Jane and I were open from day one, it's always interesting to hear other couples' stories and this one kind of blew my mind. So much so that I never want to forget it.
>
> This couple had been married for twenty years when, at her request, they decided to open up their relationship. He owned a construction company, and she was a former model. They told us about their first extramarital experience after they made this decision, and this is what kinda rocked my world.
>
> He was traveling for work in another part of the state for a few days when one morning she called him. Their gardener was a young, hot guy

whom she had secretly been wanting for a while. She asked her husband over the phone if she could take the gardener into the house and fuck him, which the husband agreed to.

I couldn't wrap my mind around the fact that this big, tough guy, who had spent his life in the construction industry, would be comfortable with his model wife fucking the gardener—someone who was at their house on a regular basis—while he was away on a business trip. To me, this seemed like diving into the deep end of a pool without ever having had a swimming lesson. I just couldn't believe it. His confidence in who he was and his ability to manage his ego was incredibly impressive to me. I have tried to exemplify his courage and strength each time I come up against a challenge that seems over my head.

Chapter 11
Pride Kills

> The night of the fight, you may feel a slight sting. That's pride fucking with you. Fuck pride. Pride only hurts, it never helps. You fight through that shit.
>
> —*Marsellus Wallace*

When Jane first told me that she was going to start a blog about her sexual exploits, to let other women know what an unabashed and self-described slut's life could be like in New York City. It didn't even register with me what that would mean, so I enthusiastically helped her with some of the technical aspects of setting up the blog. It felt good to be involved with what she was doing, but in hindsight, I should have thought a bit more about how that would impact my life.

The blog launched and Jane was immediately hooked by the creative outlet, and by the responses she was getting from readers. She enjoyed detailing all her sexual exploits in the city's underground party and sex scene, and she also found her voice as an activist, writing commentary on the rampantly sexist attitudes our culture has toward women with a high sex-drive. She was leading by example with her own life, and also interviewing sex workers and other people whose behavior society labeled as deviant.

Many of the women (and men) who found her posts were overjoyed to find out that they were not alone in their sluttery and alternative desires. Whatever the subject, her analysis came from the heart and the head. She was walking the walk and talking the talk, and people ate it up. This was not some random hot woman talking about sex—this was a doctor of psychology talking about sex and that mattered. I'm sure it didn't hurt that she was also a sexy, hot woman talking about her own sex life and telling them that their desires were okay.

> *Excerpt from Jane's blog:*
> Men often like to fancy themselves (consciously or unconsciously) sexually more powerful, dominant, and experienced than women. And we live in a world that stokes that fancy by teaching us that women are not, and should not, be highly sexual, particularly outside the context of a long-term, monogamous relationship. In such a world, being faced with a woman whose sexual desire is so vast, so strong, so licentious that it cannot be satisfied by one man is intimidating at best, terrifying at worst. Such a woman presents living, breathing, tangible proof of the seemingly impossible— female desire that is larger than male desire *and*

larger than men's ability to satisfy it. As such, she threatens to shatter men's idealized image of themselves as sexual powerhouses and destroy their sense of self.

I was all on board with her public activism except . . . it meant she was out there with her megaphone telling the world all about her sex life, which sometimes included her husband and sometimes did not.

The blog started taking on a life of its own and Jane was finding that it was a great avenue for her to reach people. As her readership grew, they became more interested in her life in general so naturally her husband became the focus of some user discussions in the comments to her posts. To give the people what they wanted, Jane started asking me to do an occasional guest blog post.

The first one I decided to write, "Coming Out as Open," described my dilemma upon being requested by a certain social media platform to confirm that I was in an open relationship with Jane. (In fact, that blog post became the starting point for this narrative.) People loved it and I too was drawn in further.

A couple months later, I wrote my second post, "A Fantasy to End All Fantasies." I described the sexual fantasy I wanted to live out more than anything, which was to have sex with Jane as a 17-year-old. Not her, though. I was 17 in the fantasy and she was 33, her age at the time.

Excerpt from Jane's blog (guest post by Adam):
I'd come across her in Central Park on my way to Sheep Meadow, where she'd be sitting on a bench reading something. I would have noticed her from far away probably, as I would any sexually provocatively woman I see. As I walk by her, she gives me a mischievous grin, and goes back to her book. I get about 20 paces away from her before I dare myself to go back and talk to her. Feigning complete confidence, which I was really a master at, I sit down next to her and say hi. We begin talking, and flirt for a good long while before I ask for her number, which surprisingly she gives me. For the rest of the afternoon, she is all I can think of while I'm hanging out with my friends. That night she is the subject of several of my fantasies and continues to be for the next few days.

That weekend we meet at a cafe and end up spending the whole afternoon together. Lunch turns to dinner and the discussion has turned very sexual as she describes her life and how she believes a woman should have as much sex as she wants. She doesn't believe in monogamy which leaves me thinking, "There are women who do that?" I'm so completely aroused by this woman—the way she looks, the way she talks—that my body is aching for her in every way. I'm 17, she's

33, and appears to me, in all seriousness, as the sex goddess of NYC. As we finish dinner, she invites me to come home with her and my head is spinning from the possibilities. This is the moment I have been waiting for since I started understanding what sex is. For the rest of the evening my life becomes the personal fantasy that has been playing out in my head for the last few years.

Jane's blog was fun for both of us and bringing us closer. She'd bounce ideas for posts off me; sometimes I'd review a post for her. But as she got more and more positive feedback from readers, she got more and more detailed about her own sex life. That meant intimate details of *my* private life were on public display for my friends and possibly even my employees who happened to follow the blog. It's one thing to know your wife is fucking other men; it's another thing entirely to have her describing it to the world every week.

Excerpt from Jane's blog:
In no time, I felt the second cock bury itself deep inside me. Oh My God. There is truly nothing like having both my holes filled by two living, breathing, pulsating cocks while my body is pressed between two beautiful men, and my clit is naturally rubbing against one of their bodies.

> Rideshare boy started fucking my ass slowly. Apollo couldn't move much in the position that he was in, but I could still feel him throbbing in my pussy. The sense of complete fullness and the overwhelming stimulation coming from every single nerve ending in my genital area sent me to a powerful orgasm that seemed to go on forever.

In my head and heart, I believed in what she was doing. I saw the devastation our culture had inflicted on women through slut shaming and through broader control of their sexuality and bodies, but it still stung. Jane never wrote anything unflattering about me specifically, and at times it was very much the opposite. Some of her posts portrayed me as quite the stallion. It was a real conflict for me.

With all sorts of details about my sex life being made public, I felt like the entire world was able to make judgments about the kind of man I was. Intellectually, I knew this was self-created crap in my head, as most people didn't care what I or my wife did. There were plenty of people who commented on her blog posts that were supportive. But some of the feedback I was getting in real life, and in the comments to her posts, let me know that judging me was exactly what some of them were doing.

One of the impetuses to start the blog was Jane's involvement in the kink world, specifically with Ronan, an undergraduate film student whom she had met up at school while she was getting her PhD. He was DJ'ing at parties and playing exactly the kind of music that Jane loved, so they became friends, and then play partners with a heavy D/s component. Jane was the Domme and Ronan the sub.

After they had been connecting for a while, he wanted to dive deep into a 24/7 D/s connection. They wrote up a contract of what that would entail and during Jane's last year at school, he served as her personal slave. Besides being her sex toy, he was contractually obligated to do anything her heart or body desired. He did all her household chores—cooking, cleaning, laundry—and slept at night in a small cage he had built up in the attic. In return, Jane completely controlled him, holding his money for him, telling him what he could and couldn't do in his daily life, and yes, imparting some hard-core physical abuse to his body and genitalia, something that they both appeared to get off on.

He would sometimes visit us for the weekend, which was one of the oddest things I had the "pleasure" of experiencing in my life with Jane. When he was at our house, he would bring us coffee in bed in the morning, cook, make our bed, and generally just do whatever chores needed to be done. The entire time he was completely naked. Jane even offered to make him suck my cock anytime I wanted, but unfortunately, that really wasn't arousing to me at all. I just wasn't into boys. It was hard not to feel sympathy for Ronan, or try to stand up for him when Jane was abusing him verbally, even though I knew this was what he wanted.

I never felt any of the jealousy with Ronan that I felt with other men. This was probably due to the fact that he was so young and so submissive that I thought of him as a child at some level. I could never consider him a threat to my relationship with Jane.

Ronan and Jane would go to kink parties together, which I would attend too, but purely as a voyeur. I could get into a little kink with my submissive lovers, some spanking, rope bondage, and forced sexual engagement (consensual non-consent, as its sometimes called), but nothing like how Jane and Ronan expressed themselves. In fact, the disparity was so large that Jane would often introduce me as her "vanilla" husband. I joked that I was a man without a country, as my vanilla friends thought I was kinky, and my kinky friends thought I was vanilla.

Jane and Ronan's antics and public performances at these kink parties were a big part of her blog, prompting a lot of people to assume that I was part of that connection, or that Jane controlled me as well. On more than one occasion someone would come up to me at one of these kink parties and say how lucky I was to be married to my Domme, which was always weird. I could see the disappointment in their eyes when I told them that our connection was completely egalitarian.

I was able to shrug off these assumptions and conversations with medium success, always keeping in mind that I didn't want someone to think he doth protest too much and I really *was* a sub in bed. But when the public "cuck" comments started, I really began to struggle with my self-image.

The cuck thing seemed to overwhelm the entire narrative for me. It's like a variation on the old joke: "You can build a thousand houses, but if your wife fucks a few hundred guys . . . do they call you a house builder?"

What was it about the word *cuck* that really got at me? I thought back to my childhood, when we used the word *fag* in the same sort of way—as a put-down of men or boys we perceived as deficient in the masculinity department. I certainly renounce that behavior of mine, but I was young, and it was a long time ago, living in a less evolved world.

All the same, that childhood instinct was still there. And apparently it was still important to me that everyone knew I was the right kind of man, a strong man, a real man. And every time Jane shared her sexual activities with other men in a blog post, every time I got called a cuck, it was a little blow to my pride. Kind of like death by a thousand paper cuts.

I had a lot of discussions with myself about where this pain was coming from. I felt like other guys were laughing at me. I felt like I was getting notched down in the grand social competition of life. It seemed I had found the limits of my newfound theory of competition, in that when I added a stadium of spectators, I started to feel their eyes and the weight of their judgment upon me

Even before I had met Jane, I had worked hard to move away from relying on validation from other people, and I'd made real progress, but these experiences made it clear how much work I still had to do. The power that the word *cuck* had over me was evidence of that.

Jane and I had an open relationship, open-as-fuck, but did that mean I *was* a cuck? When other men called me that, was it true? In reality I was probably more masculine than the guys calling me names—especially by *their* measure of masculinity, which was inevitably tied to the number of conquests notched on their bedpost. During my days as a college athlete, I knew a lot of these types, and the locker-room talk was an odd mixture of toxic masculinity and homoeroticism.

My egalitarian, open relationship did not make me a cuck. I was sure of that. But what would make me cuck? I had to admit I didn't really know exactly what a cuck was, I mean I had an idea, but that was mostly based on how the term was used in pop culture.

Now, I wasn't a social scientist who studied human sexuality by any stretch of the imagination, but luckily enough I did happen to live with one. In my efforts to understand the "cuck" thing, I ended up speaking with Jane at length about it. Not about my own failings of course. I broached the topic with her from a "scientific curiosity" angle.

Act III, Scene 96
Jane and Adam are sitting on the couch drinking coffee.

ADAM: Hey, I wanted to ask you. You know how that guy was calling me out on your post from last week?

JANE: You know, I never look at the comments.

ADAM: Hmm . . . probably wise. Anyway, this idiot was ranting that your husband is a total cuck.

JANE: Ha! That's kind of funny.

ADAM: Yeah right? But I realized I don't actually know what a cuck truly is from a sexual kink perspective.

JANE: Well, it's when a man gets sexually aroused by the idea or reality of his partner being with another man, so he'd want to hear about it in full detail afterward. Possibly even get videos and pictures of it, or be present and watch. "Cuckquean" is used for women who enjoy their partners being with others, but it's used much less frequently. Anyway, unfortunately for me, you are definitely not a cuck, cause that would be sooo hot.

ADAM, *slyly with a smile*: Got it, and sorry to be such a disappointment for you.

(*Jane laughs and kisses Adam on the cheek.*)

JANE: You know I love you just the way you are. I'd only change one or two things, tops. Maybe three.

ADAM: I love you too sweetie. . . . So, you're a cuck if it turns you on?

JANE: Yes basically, though there are different ways of going about it. For some, it comes packaged with a component of sexual submission and humiliation. For others, it's just a pure sexual turn-on without any BDSM power dynamics. It all depends on the individual and the couple.

ADAM: That's so funny. This happened to me with Bryce and her boyfriend José. You know that little blonde snowboarder I ride with? I introduced you at a party a couple of months ago. She once made José watch while I fucked her. She even threw a few put-downs at him.

JANE: Wait, José was that big guy, right? The surfer from Southern California. I remember thinking he was kind of an asshole.

ADAM: Yeah, that's him. I think it's safe to put him in the "cuck who likes to watch—with a humiliation component" category.

JANE: Wow. Didn't see that coming. I like him a lot more now that I know he's in touch with his submissive side.

ADAM: Interesting, eh?

JANE: With that in mind, here is some more data for you. According to some scientific research, knowing your partner has been with another man, whether in a cuckolding situation or not, prompts a biological response that gives men the ability to have longer and more vigorous sex. This often results in harder orgasms, a higher sperm count, and a shorter refractory period between hard-ons.

ADAM: Well, those all sound like pretty good benefits to me.

Thinking about my experience with José and Bryce, I marveled at how José was this big, tough guy whose place in the org chart of Southern California surfing depended on his image as someone nobody wanted to cross. Get the fuck off my wave or

I'll beat the shit out of you was his mentality. Obviously being a cuck, not to mention a sub, had zero relevance to his position on the masculinity continuum, which was way over on the Bro side of things. His masculinity was defined by his public behavior and his reputation within his peer group, which I was not a part of. I assume this played into the reason I was chosen to join them.

These data points led me to conclude that being a cuck was no more associated with any particular position on my bland-to-toxic masculinity continuum than being dominant, submissive, gay, or straight. They're kinks and orientations, not a measure of one's masculinity.

Even knowing all this, the word *cuck* continued to have a strange hold on me. Years after I was going through all this, I became quite friendly with a colleague of Jane's, a successful psychology professor and a published author. He and his stripper wife (she also happens to have a doctorate in psychology, but it's more fun to say "stripper wife" than "postdoc wife") are totally open about their non-monogamy.

Because he had a very public profile, he routinely got called a cuck on his social media feeds, so I chatted with him about the subject. He admitted to me that even though most of the men doing it were ignorant bullies and trolls, their words had a real effect on him. I fully identified with that feeling and really wished I'd known him back when Jane's blog was taking off.

It wasn't my choice to have this public persona, and I would go back and forth between being excited and made uneasy by it. Given my desire to get comfortable with being uncomfortable, I was in the sweet spot, and in general enjoying it, since processing the conflicting feelings was continuing to promote growth in me.

Then one day I got a call from a woman who I had been getting into a light D/s connection with. She questioned me quite aggressively if I was secretly a sub and whether I liked pegging. Surprised, I said no, I wasn't a sub and was curious why she asked about pegging. The phone went silent for a moment. Then I was told I should probably go check out Jane's latest post.

Act III, Scene 145

Jane is working at her desk in the spare bedroom. Adam enters the room.

ADAM: We need to talk.

JANE: What about?

ADAM: I need you to take down that post about fucking me in the ass with a strap-on.

JANE: Why?

ADAM: It's too personal. I'm not comfortable with something that intimate being blasted out for the whole world to see. Additionally, I don't think you represented it correctly. It's a thing we've done a couple times, but you talked about it as if it was something we do all the time, which isn't true.

JANE: Well, I could change that part but it's worth noting you didn't seem to mind when I talked about how much I love watching women suck your perfect cock.

ADAM: Yeah, okay, but going forward if you're going to be talking about me on your blog you really need to check with me first.

JANE: Well, I'm not okay with that. You'll just pick and choose the things that support your existing paradigm of how you think a man should be.

ADAM: I think you know me better than that.

JANE: Do I? Can I leave the post up?

ADAM: No. Please take it down. I'm not comfortable with it.

JANE, *getting agitated*: Are you fucking kidding me? I wouldn't have thought a little pegging would threaten your masculinity this much. What is wrong with all you homophobic American men?

We went back and forth for a while before Jane stormed out of the apartment, saying that she couldn't be with a man who had hang-ups like I did. That hurt. I knew that I was pushing myself to be with her, and to have all my effort erased in an instant like that hurt badly. When Jane came back the next day, she apologized and took the post down. She wasn't happy about it though.

I'm not entirely comfortable bringing it up here either but the lens of time is a funny thing, and I'm curious if I'm doing it just to fuck with my younger self. Boys can be brutal to each other but it's a sign of love. More likely, I'm doing it because it still scares me to share it, so therefore I have to. There is a part of me that feels emasculated by it, and while intellectually I know that's ridiculous, it's still hard to shake.

While I disagreed with Jane about how she went about it, she was spot-on about my wanting to protect my insecurities. But it's not homophobia that made me feel uncomfortable. It was the idea of the world thinking I'm a sub in bed. This was confirmed by the fact that the woman who had alerted me to it said she was going to have a hard time thinking of me as dominant going forward. Apparently, her friends were laughing at her "boyfriend" getting fucked in the ass. That blog post of Jane's struck right at the heart of the masculinity debate, and the whole social pecking order of life. It was evident from this incident how much I still bought into the hierarchical masculinity paradigm.

I didn't care how many people knew that I fucked Jane in the ass, but my pride couldn't handle the world knowing that she had fucked me in the ass. It's hard to admit even now, but here I am. I've laid so much of myself out on the table at this point, holding anything back would seem counter to the entire project. The silver lining was that it was another experience forcing me to detach what the world thinks of my masculinity from my own personal sense of who I am.

Side Effects of Public Non-monogamy May Include . . .

As Jane's academic and social media career continued to grow, we routinely attended events at universities and conference centers related to her research. I enjoyed joining her on these excursions quite a bit. It was a chance to rub elbows with some fascinating folks that I normally wouldn't encounter in my everyday life.

Frequently, Jane's reputation preceded her, and given how public Jane was about both her sexuality and mine, when people met me, they knew they had a sympathetic ear when it came to matters of the flesh.

At one event we attended on the West Coast, Jane and I were introduced to a superinteresting couple, Jim and Niesha. He was a well-known professor in the area and a celebrated author who had written several critically acclaimed books. He routinely showed up on news programs in his subject matter of expertise. Niesha was also a professor and highly regarded in her field, though she did not have the public persona that her husband did. Jim was brilliant and vibrant and looked to live life to the fullest. Niesha was dynamic and engaging and the two of them had what appeared to be such a relaxed loving energy between them.

We all chatted for a while at the event, until at one point in the evening I found myself talking one-on-one with Niesha, who, I'll add as a side note, was stunningly beautiful. She brought up the subject of non-monogamy and wondered if I would be interested in meeting up with her. We chatted a bit more in a flirty way, and then she asked whether it would be okay with me if Jim came and watched us, but without participating. She had been feeling me out the whole time to see if I would be open to engaging with them in their cuckolding kink. Here I was now getting propositioned to participate in the very thing that that had been causing me so much stress. On top of it, Jim was a guy I instantly liked (unlike the surfer José).

Jim liked watching Niesha have sex with other guys, and Niesha liked having him watch—quite the symbiotic kink. But if you have a highly public reputation at a top university and in the mainstream media, you're taking a risk every time you invite a man into your sex life. You need to be sure he's trustworthy, not to mention someone who understands the nature of what you want. Niesha, it seemed, was the advance scout for their escapades.

Given how attracted I was to Niesha and that I like weird sex things, I agreed. We couldn't make it work while Jane and I were on that trip, so they ended up meeting me at my place in

Colorado and making a weekend out of it. The three of us had a fun time together.

I can certainly empathize with Jim and Niesha. Our culture's prejudices and their own success have made it harder for them to live a life with the excitement they want. Being able to participate in a small way to their life satisfaction was a beautiful thing, and since then I have relished the chance to do the same for other couples. It was a wonderful, unanticipated benefit from my public, open-as-fuck relationship—and something Jane loved hearing about in detail. One of the few times I was able to completely usurp all of our share time together was after my night with Jim and Niesha. Jane sat rapt while I recounted first the dinner, then drinks at a cocktail bar, with lots of flirting between Niesha and me. Finally, at Jim's suggestion, we went back to my place.

It was there that Jim became a shadow. Niesha and I started making out and lightly dancing to some Portishead I had put on. I slipped the straps of her dress off her shoulders and it fell to the floor. Niesha was standing before me in nothing but some sexy lingerie. I picked her up, carried her into the bedroom, and laid her down on the bed. As she began to remove my shirt I caught a glimpse of Jim just outside the bedroom door, looking in.

While I was aware of Jim's presence, I never really heard or saw him till it was all over. It was a delicious experience, and Jane was so aroused hearing the details that she totally jumped me when I was done.

***

Early on, I realized that if I wanted to be with Jane, I was going to have to celebrate her sexuality. That wasn't always easy. But it was good to remind myself of the advantages of having a sex-positive partner. Jane always encouraged me to try any kinks or desires I might have, or just wanted to explore. I thought about Jim and Niesha. He has a kink that society, for the most part, finds repugnant, but fortunately his partner has empathy and understanding for his desires. In fact, she's aroused by them and willingly participates in fulfilling them. Our culture would think of Niesha as a slut and look down on her just because she enjoys casual sex. And happens to enjoy it while her husband watches.

I have known a good number of self-described sluts, and I love the way they are taking back that word from all the haters. That men's reputations benefit from sexual promiscuity while women's suffer for it is one of the great tragedies of our culture. Our collective happiness and sex lives have suffered immeasurably because of it.

Women who are sex-forward live their lives the way they want to in the face of significant cultural pressures. That is highly attractive to me. I want the experience-hunter girlfriend who just doesn't give a shit what people think or say about her sexuality, which is how I want to live. It's something I am continually striving for. Sometimes finding that internal validation was easy, and sometimes it was hard. At times I failed, but after putting myself out there, or getting put out there by Jane, time and again, it got easier.

I began to understand that my place on the bland-to-toxic masculinity continuum was dependent on me and my behavior alone, and not on how the world viewed me, my wife, or our relationship. My whole life, I had been battling the image I had of myself as the geeky, uncool redheaded kid on the playground, and I was always fighting to prove to the world that I wasn't that kid. I was always looking to what other people thought of me (or what I thought they thought of me) for evidence that I'd succeeded.

I needed to recognize that I was already behaving in the ways that the man I wanted to be would behave. I was already doing what I had to do to be that man. I didn't need second-party validation. Every morning when I looked in the mirror, there was this ripped guy with broad shoulders, muscular arms, and a full beard, but part of me still saw that geeky, frail, unpopular redheaded kid. Jane's blog pushed me to realize that the kid I saw wasn't actually there.

Our relationship forced me to admit I was becoming exactly who I wanted to be. A Fierce Gentleman who stands up for those who can't stand up for themselves, a protector, a competitor, a guy who fixes his own truck and has rebuilt several houses. A guy who's got "not *that* big" big dick energy, but also the confidence to show emotions, be vulnerable, and admit when he's wrong.

> *Excerpt from Jane's blog:*
> Unlike me, [Adam] does feel jealousy and does have insecurities, and he needs rules to reassure him of our connection and his place in my heart.

As he's become more secure in our relationship, he feels more and more comfortable relaxing some of his constraints on me, but there are still many left.

For now, it suffices to say that I have agreed to let him slowly grow into my level of openness because he's the closest to my ideal partner I've ever met, and he's shown willingness to venture out beyond his comfort zone.

So far, I haven't regretted my decision. Although my freedom is somewhat curtailed, I have plenty of maneuvering space. Enough to keep me satisfied. Enough so, that the other benefits of being in this relationship outweigh the costs of not having complete, absolute freedom. And then there is the hope that my freedoms will grow over time.

Chapter 12
Growing into the Relationship That Jane Wanted

Excerpt from Adam's journal:
The night before the climb I couldn't sleep. I was nervous. I was scared. For years I had fantasized about climbing Slipstream, the northeast edge of Mount Snow Dome, one of the most beautiful lines to behold. It just begged to be climbed. I tried to imagine what it would be like on that edge with the entire glacial valley spread out below me. A route like that seemed like the entire reason I got into climbing. But even thinking about being on the route scared me. It's a three-thousand-foot vertical obstacle course of steep rock, ice, and snow. Not to mention you're a sitting duck under a hanging glacier and avalanche slopes for the entire climb, so the faster you can climb, the safer you are. I questioned if I was good enough, fast enough.

My climbing partner and I woke to perfect weather and the sun was coming up in a cloudless sky as we hiked up the two-mile moraine to the start of the climb. Dropping our packs, we stared up at the intimidating wall towering above us. We were in the pause, that moment when everything is unknown. There was only this mountain and us. The rest of the world had faded away.

In silence we roped up, both of us in our own thoughts about what we were doing, and then we began. From the start we were moving very well. The climbing felt easy to us, and after about a thousand feet of feeling good and being in the flow zone, we decided to simul-climb—both of us moving at the same time while tied to opposite ends of the rope—to double our speed. The ice, rock and snow kept passing, and we kept going up. It was easy, it was fun, it was going so well. We were having the best day.

And then, before we knew it, we were at the final headwall of ice, which ended up being an easy sneak up through a huge crack in the hanging glacier. Three and half hours after we started, we were standing on the top. It had been a joy, pure fun, and not even half as stressful as I had been imagining. I had built it up into a monster, when really all I needed to do was give it the respect it deserved and have trust in my ability.

Act III, Scene 285

It's evening. Adam is in the kitchen cooking dinner. Jane is sitting on the couch in the living room.

JANE: Hey sweetheart, I'd like to discuss starting to make some changes to our arrangement.

(*Adam puts down the knife and turns to look at Jane.*)

JANE: I'd like to have a hookup when you're home. Are you ready for this?

(*Long pause.*)

ADAM: Yeah, I guess the time has come, and in answer to your question, I have no idea if I'm ready for it.

JANE: Well, you always said you would try to get to this point, and we've been doing it your way for a while now.

ADAM: It wasn't "my way." It was a compromise that took me out of my comfort zone but in a way that I felt I could manage.

JANE: True.

ADAM: But you're right, it was always meant as a waypoint to being more open.

JANE: What's your hesitation?

ADAM: I don't think I'm comfortable discussing my deep emotional shit with a developmental psychologist who also happens to be my wife.

JANE, *laughing*: Okay, well then, how are we going to proceed? How can you get comfortable with this?

ADAM: I don't know. I mean, I knew at some point I was going to have to cross this boundary, so perhaps we just proceed with it slowly and see how it goes.

JANE: You know you've always been able to hook up with someone one-on-one when we're both here. I was fine with you doing that.

ADAM: Yes, I know, but I couldn't do that while also asking you not to. I would have had a hard time feeling good about who I was with that arrangement.

JANE: Understood, but what I was hoping is that you would hook up and see that it's no big deal, then you could relax that constraint. So, perhaps it's time for you to explore this too?

ADAM: Apparently it is.

Honestly, it was a bit frustrating. Here I was, finally in a good, comfortable space with Jane and her exploits, and I would have been happy to keep the arrangement the way it was. But she had a point: the "temporary compromise" had been in place for a few years now. Pushing back just so I could stay comfortable wasn't in my nature, and also meant that Jane wasn't where she wanted to be.

Emotionally, it felt like I was being rushed into something I didn't want to do, but this had been the plan all along. This had already been agreed upon. I knew that I was never going to be completely fine with Jane's desire to have a relationship that allowed sex anytime, anywhere, with anyone, but if I could get comfortable with something that we could both live with, it gave us a better chance of continuing together. I loved this relationship, I loved Jane, so I had to try.

After four years together, we had built up a solid foundation of trust between us, and good on Jane for her patience. I also saw that when I pushed a rule and then decided it was too far, Jane was okay with pulling it back. I think just making the effort went a long way with her, and I appreciated that. So here I was again, going to the uncomfortable place.

Jane's focus was on novelty, so most of her hookups were one-offs. But she did have a few repeat customers and decided to use one of them for this first foray into the unknown, since time and place could be much more easily controlled with confidence. After confirmation from bachelor number 729, it was all set up to take place in three days.

In the days leading up to the evening I was apprehensive. It was almost sure to be a very difficult evening for me. Each night I slept less. Forefront in my brain was the vivid memory of the night and day I spent alone during the Sophie foursome. I did not want to go through that again, and I found myself slipping into negativity throughout the day, talking out loud to no one, asking "How many guys does she need to fuck?" and "Why am I always the one having to push my boundaries?" Why couldn't she let me get bored with the situation so that exploring was exciting too, not just scary? I was distracted from my work, and the basic functions of life like going to the supermarket or doing the laundry seemed overwhelming.

The day arrived and I kind of meandered my way through the daylight hours, always busy but not really accomplishing anything. I kept waiting for the sledgehammer to hit me. I kept waiting for that punch to land, the one that would collapse me into a ball of angst and agitation.

Jane had decided she would go straight from her office to the evening, which I felt would be easier. As darkness fell, a familiar pattern of thoughts began to invade me. I was a weak man. I should have pushed back and refused to explore this type of connection. But the three years of work I had done started to pay off. I stopped the thinking in its tracks and just took a few long, slow breaths. In through the nose, out through the mouth. Calmly, I stepped out of my head, took a good hard look at myself, and then laughed. My brain telling me that I was weak was a foolish argument. In fact, I could easily reason it was the exact opposite, that I was pushing my boundaries because I'm strong enough to do it.

Once again, fear was trying to gain the upper hand and take me to a dark place, but I found that I no longer needed to go along with it. To prove it to myself, I looked straight into the monster's eyes and said out loud: "Jane is out fucking another guy." I sat quietly. I felt something, but wasn't exactly sure what. I recognized that I was a bit lonely. I would have preferred that she wasn't out fucking another guy, but she was, and that was that. Eventually, I got up to make some dinner. I could have ordered something, but I wanted to cook. It felt good to be active in the apartment.

The waiting was over, the monster had arrived, and I chose to see that it wasn't real. It was telling, and par for the course with me, to see how my thoughts had shifted over time from the false narrative of "Jane is going to find out the truth about me" to the false narrative of "This is going to make me look weak because I didn't push back." Once again, my brain was trying to find a way to undermine my self-confidence. Like water always working its way to the lowest level by the easiest path, my thoughts flowed to a different weakness in my psyche to try and work its way through. I wondered if my brain would ever stop fucking with me.

As I passed the rest of the evening in the apartment, everything felt so normal. Her scarves hanging on the wall were just scarves; the coffee table was as boring and meaningless as it always was. I was comfortable just being there, watching something stupid while sitting on our shitty Ikea furniture. There was an article in a climbing magazine about a good friend Sara up in Canada who was pushing the limits of what a human could do, so I read it. I even did some coding work on the software.

I got into bed at 10:30 and around 11, I got the text "headed home" followed by a heart emoji. I looked at the text and just smiled, immediately going back to whatever I was watching. Twenty-five minutes later I heard her keys in the door. Jane was home. I lay there in the stillness of our bedroom, wondering how this would go.

"You up?" she asked from the kitchen.

"Yep!" I responded.

She poked her head in the bedroom door and said with a smile, "I'll be right in."

I could hear her go into the bathroom and start the shower. Ten minutes later she returned, put on her sleeping things, crawled into bed with me, and, without saying a word, slid under the covers and wrapped her mouth around me.

She was happy, and I felt a closeness between us at that moment—her very giving reconnection after the escapade was perfect. We had crossed a boundary that had seemed impassable to me for so long, and it felt okay.

I had been so intimidated by being home alone that night and had built up the monster into something I wasn't going to be able to control. The negative emotions based on a false narrative came, but I defused them effectively. The intense reactions I was fearing and expecting never materialized. Perhaps it was that I knew she'd be coming home; perhaps it was that our lives were so entwined in so many ways that I felt comfortable about our near-term prospects; perhaps it was that we'd been hanging out for the last two weeks solid since I had come back from out west, and a night doing my own thing felt good. Or perhaps, if I allowed myself to believe it, I had gotten to such a grounded place that the monsters no longer had the same sort of control over my thoughts as they used to. I could look at them and say, "You're not real, and you don't have any power over me anymore."

The fact that the relationship felt secure played a major part as well. I knew Jane, and she knew me. We were a team and that felt great. I was feeling confident in myself in just the ways that Jane really appreciated.

After the success of that first foray, I was willing to try it again, especially if I got an "on the house reconnection" every time she went out (which I think we both understood to be a reaffirmation of our bond and an indication of her desire to keep me in her life). A few months later, after perhaps the fourth time, it had become just another thing, and I needed less of a formal event around it. The reconnections became part of the routine, one that I highly recommend.

As a side note, when the reverse happened, Jane got an on-the-house back rub. She didn't really need aftercare the way I initially did, but she *loves* back rubs, so it was a good way to show appreciation and connection and have some kind of an attempt at balance.

> *Excerpt from Adam's journal:*
>
> My climbing partner and I are at 19,000 feet, descending off the north face of Huandoy Sur in northern Peru, completely encased in clouds. We have maybe 100 feet of visibility, and we are starting to navigate our way down a 4,250-foot face in 200-foot hops to our base camp below.
>
> At this moment, I am in the lead, staring down into the haze, trying to figure out where the best down-climbing route is, when the clouds clear for a few seconds, and I can see the entire mountain face that we had climbed that day stretched out below me. I see the glacier we had started from, and I see our base camp situated in the middle of it.
>
> The vertigo is intense. Imagine standing at the top of a staircase 4,250 feet high and 1,000 feet wide. (For comparison, the Empire State Building's observation deck is 1,250 feet high.)

The stairs are really uneven, there is no handrail, and it's as steep as a ladder placed against the side of a building. The impact of seeing the full journey, every inch of elevation, how massive the undertaking was, gives me pause in a way I have never felt before. I am humbled by the power of the mountain.

Only because of all the training and effort my partner and I had gone through to reach that spot, high up on a remote mountain in Peru, was that perspective possible. To this day, we talk about that moment in hushed whispers.

On one occasion out west, I went out with a couple who had found me through one of the apps in their search for a threesome —their first try at bringing another man into the bedroom with them.

We met for a drink and chatted about our experiences with open relationships. They were a bit younger than I was, total noobies, and since this was now five years into my relationship with Jane, it was fun to feel like I was on the other side of the experience divide. The woman was excited about being with two men and he seemed aroused by the idea as well.

We talked for about an hour, finished our drinks, and said goodbye, leaving things open for the time being. Presumably, they decided that I was up to their standards, because they called me about an hour after we parted and asked if they could come over.

We had another drink back at my place and began to awkwardly get involved with each other. Slowly, everyone relaxed and soon enough we were involved in a melee of naked bodies and carnal pleasure. She was loving it, having two cocks to play with, and having two men paying attention to her.

Fast-forward to the end of the evening, when we all woke up to the reality that in a situation like that you're always playing with fire. She was on all fours sucking my cock and her boyfriend was fucking her from behind, when I let her know I was about to climax, which is always the respectful thing to do when someone is sucking your cock for the first time and you're unaware of their comfort level. She responded to my warning by sliding me as far into her mouth as she could get me. So I just kept going and came in her mouth, which she seemed to be fully enthusiastic about.

As I regained awareness from my postorgasmic bliss, I noticed how quiet it had gotten in the room. There were some tense, hushed whispers, and then the eruption happened. He started screaming that they hadn't talked at all about her being able to do that. I sat there stunned as I watched a huge, completely naked fight blow up between them. The evening ended up being a disaster, and I felt bad for them as it had been a superfun night up to that point. I recognized myself in that experience and how close I had probably come to a similar outcome. It was a firsthand glimpse of how far I had traveled on my journey and how much I had learned along the way.

Sometimes the Frog Notices

Over the next six months, Jane and I settled into the flow of our life with our newly relaxed rules, but I noticed that we were starting to spend less and less time together. Initially, her hookups when I was home didn't happen a lot. If I spent a couple of weeks in New York, it happened once a trip. And it was giving me some freedom I hadn't allowed myself before—going on a fun date while I was in the city, so I was getting into it.

It was a slow change but by the end of that year, Jane was going on a date a week, and while I wasn't nearly at her rate, I did notice that I was also making an effort to see more women. As we started hooking up more with other people one-on-one, we began to drift apart. It wasn't immediate, and it wasn't dramatic, but slowly, over time, something was changing.

My comfort with her lifestyle had arrived at a place I hadn't been sure I was ever going to get to, but with this newfound awareness about my sense of self, I started thinking about what I had been through and where we were going. As I stepped outside myself and looked at it all, I started to see the signs of instability that I had been ignoring.

I also began to notice how many nights I was going to bed alone in our apartment. One of the foundations of our connection was how much we enjoyed being with each other when I was home in NYC. But that seemed to be getting less important to Jane. Fully opening up our relationship happened to coincide with both our careers starting to take a lot of our attention. This in theory should be a good thing, but with all the hookups, it was starting to create less space for us as a couple. Our evenings together were getting fewer.

Added to that, Jane's social media personality was starting to take on a life of its own, and the persona she created sometimes conflicted with the person who I thought I was in a relationship with. She started doing online Periscope broadcasts, almost daily. Her live feed was drawing thousands of viewers, but it was also starting to intrude into the flow of our daily life at home. It seemed to me that the woman who never gave a fuck about what people thought was now measuring everything she was doing according to whether it would increase or decrease her viewership. She was structuring her life around her social media popularity, and I started feeling like a prop in her quest for relevance as the internet's celebrity master of sex. The secure feeling that I had regarding our relationship was slipping away from me.

I was still having as much crazy wild sex as I could have wanted, but now I was able to start seeing what my emotional needs were. I had been hiding a lot of my feelings during our relationship, and that, I found, had been wearing me out. I wanted a partner who thought being with me on adventures was better than not being with me on them. I wanted a partner who put me first and who I put first—or at least second, after our careers, which was acceptable to me for short periods of time. It was becoming more and more apparent that this wasn't the case with Jane anymore.

Around that time I had started up a casual relationship with Bobby, a woman who lived near me out west. After six years with

Jane, I did not realize how starved I had been for emotional intimacy until I started spending time with someone who was giving it to me. Slowly, Bobby and I grew closer and at some point I realized it was no longer just a fun sexual connection. I was falling in love with her. To complicate matters further, she had no real experience with non-monogamy and was in way over her head now that she was involved with me, and therefore, by association, with Jane.

In a switch of roles, Bobby asked that if we were going to be together, I had to stop all other physical connections with anyone but her when I was out west. Her tender, caring, and loving way with me was so rejuvenating that I willingly agreed. The problem that I somehow chose push to the side was that Bobby continually shamed me for my past, and for the present experiences that Jane and I shared when I was back in New York. It seemed like I was back at square one again. I was feeling like the sexual freak, and feeling like I had to hide parts of myself. But her emotional connection to me was so addictive in my starved state, that I continued on.

Like an amateur backcountry skier, I was ignoring these signs of instability with Bobby just as I had with Jane.

Without intending to, I found myself in a relationship with two very different women, in two very different cities. On the surface that sounds rather perfect, but the realities of it were extraordinarily complicated. I was now officially in a polyamorous configuration. I loved Jane and had a depth of shared experience with her, and we had a strong bond, but now I was splitting the energy I had to express my love between two women, which I willingly tried to do.

On top of that, I started to adjust my behavior with Jane, having to hide much of what went on with me and Jane in NYC from any social media exposure because Bobby didn't want to know anything about it. It was painful to her, which in hindsight probably should have been something that made me realize this was not a healthy situation for either Bobby or me to be in. Obviously not sustainable.

Splitting my love and trying to tap-dance around the realities of my life was exhausting. I didn't do it very well and probably did a disservice to both Jane and Bobby, although mostly Bobby, as I should have been more sensitive to how far out of her comfort zone she was with non-monogamy.

In the end Bobby and I fell apart, but our relationship showed me how much I needed a partner who prioritized me, a partner who allowed me to be human with normal human emotions. It also showed me how much I did get from Jane, a partner who didn't shame me for my sexual desires or past experiences. I wanted a partner who celebrated me the way I celebrated her, who found happiness in my expression to the rest of the world whatever way I chose to explore it.

I also learned that I'm not polyamorous and have no desire to be that close to two partners ever again. I don't have the energy for it, and it took away from my time and desire to enjoy the things in life that feed my soul. Hell, it's hard enough having one relationship, I don't know how I thought I could do two.

In all fairness to Jane, she was completely supportive of my involvement with Bobby and was totally fine with my being poly while she was simply partnered with sexual openness. It's unclear to me if this was due to her desiring me to be happy or because it gave her more freedom, which seemed to accelerate our slide apart.

***

When I got into the relationship with Jane, I hid my feelings about her lifestyle because I didn't trust them, as I sensed they were based on false narratives that had plagued me since I was young. I also had to hide them because Jane saw them as weakness. And to be honest, I don't like showing weakness, especially to women. But I started to understand that it's not weakness to admit what my needs are. In fact, it's the only way to open the door to growing closer with your partner.

After Bobby left, I found myself still in a relationship with intelligent, sexy, adventurous Jane, who seemed to be getting more and more absent emotionally. Or had I been so blinded by desire, always looking at the signs of stability that I wanted to see, that I ignored the fault lines that had been there all along? It wasn't sustainable like this, or at least I wasn't interested in putting in the effort anymore if she wasn't.

Chapter 13
All Journeys End

Excerpt from Adam's journal:
I slowly open my eyes to see the soft light of the predawn sky streaming through the high windows of my bedroom at the foot of the Rocky Mountains.

I lie in bed, silent and still, watching the clear winter day brighten as the sun gets ever closer to breaching the horizon. Sometimes a particularly spectacular sunrise bathes the room in orange, but today it's just the warmth of the yellow sun as the first rays come through the east-facing windows.

I'm alone. I've been alone for the last year and a half, stuck here while the pandemic rages.

But I've been making it through a journey of solitude that seemed impossible when I first started, to a world I thought I could never go to.

It was 2020 and the pandemic was raging. Jane and I had broken up. Our relationship had started unraveling almost two years earlier and came apart completely in late 2019. Initially, I spent almost as much time as I could in the backcountry taking risks with my snowboarding, working out my pain from losing Jane, and then shortly thereafter, losing the social life I'd known to the virus.

The first summer of the pandemic, after the snows had melted, I was a bit adrift. I had no real work to speak of, and everything in the world outside was on hold. Jane was in the apartment in Brooklyn, I was in the Rocky Mountain retreat, and we hadn't really spoken in eight months. I was alone and had lots of free time to explore whatever my heart desired.

Turns out, what my heart desired was to learn how to play the electric guitar. I went online and bought an old, beat-up Fender Stratocaster because I liked the way it looked.

Sitting on the floor of my living room, in front of the old stone fireplace, surrounded by all the torn-up bubble-wrap and packaging, I held the guitar in my hands and saw possibilities in front of me.

***

When Jane and I finally admitted that the relationship was over, we continued living together but moved into separate bedrooms. I appreciated the company and the rent payment. Occasionally, we would still have sex with each other, even trading a back rub for a blowjob until that too went away. There was most definitely a piece of me that was hoping that we were just going through a phase, and we would come back together in a way that was better, but eventually that desire faded too.

After a year or so of living with this arrangement, we had a particularly ugly two months. We decided we needed some separation, and that it was best for her to move out. In one of our last face-to-face talks during the ugliness before I left to go spend some time out west, Jane asked me if I wished I had never met her. There was no hesitation on my part in answering that there wasn't any piece of me that felt that way. There were so many wonderful things about the relationship, and so much personal growth, that I shudder at the thought of having missed out on it all.

The plan was, I would go out west to stay in the house till she found a place and then I would come back to the Brooklyn apartment. Two months later the pandemic hit. She was stuck in our apartment, unable to move out, and I was stuck in Colorado.

***

As I started learning how to play the blues on the Stratocaster, I tapped into my experience with Jane and what we had been through together. The ending had been so unsatisfyingly unspectacular. It was like I wanted it to have blown apart in a fiery explosion so that I could feel the sharpness of the pain. The way it faded almost felt like an insult. This relationship meant so much to me and we just drifted apart. It seems impossible but it was true.

My drift had started when I began recognizing my own emotional needs for the first time. Jane had been clear about her needs from day one, and I had not really known what mine were, so I rolled with hers. I can see that my decision-making was influenced by my infatuation with her and her crazy lifestyle. It may not have been the healthiest thing, even though it was a lot of fun. I started to ask if maybe the relationship she wanted wasn't the one I wanted.

With the old rules lifted, Jane's hookups slowly began to feel like a constant intrusion into our life. I had a hard time wrapping my brain around her level of activity, and we began to move away from each other emotionally. We stopped taking trips together; she stopped coming out west to snowboard and climb; we even stopped doing so many of the things we loved doing together in NYC.

As she dove harder into her lifestyle, I started to feel like I wasn't a priority to her anymore. I still loved Jane, but I began to see that she wasn't loving me the way I wanted. It felt like she was taking me for granted and I became less and less willing to keep doing my part to support the relationship. I wondered if perhaps she had been taking me for granted all along, and I had been choosing to ignore it.

We were living together but it seemed like we were doing so out of habit. Jane let go of the relationship without letting go of me, and when the relationship stopped being a priority for her, I started looking elsewhere.

Act III, Final Scene
It's early evening. Jane is dressed to go out. She is putting her shoes on. Adam watches her.

ADAM: Is this over? Are we done?

JANE: I think so, yes.

(Jane opens the door of the apartment and leaves.)

***

Almost a year into the pandemic, still without much work, I was in the backcountry four days a week and playing guitar almost every day. I wasn't necessarily happy, but I was living, and living far better than could be expected given the circumstances of the world, and that mattered. Being alone has always been difficult for me, but given that there was no real choice, I leaned into it. I made improvements to the house by creating new light fixtures out of reclaimed materials, and got deeper into my cooking in the beautiful kitchen I had built. I took guitar lessons off of YouTube.

Around this time, a friend came out west to snowboard with me. He and his wife of 20 years had opened up their marriage, and he asked me questions about how Jane and I had made it work so smoothly. I laughed, and said it wasn't always so smooth for me and began to tell him the story, recounting as much as I could over the next two days. He was fascinated by it and encouraged me to write it down. After he left, I thought about that. Given that the pandemic still had me without work and alone, and I seemed to suck at writing songs, I started writing the story. It was surprisingly cathartic, so I just kept going.

***

My climbing partner of twenty years and I finally stopped climbing together a few years ago. We had been gradually pushing our limits on big mountains for years, and on our final trip together, we very nearly summited the biggest mountain we had ever tried to climb but turned back at the last minute because for me, the risk had become too great, and I had had enough. I decided I was done with that mountain and was ready to head down to safety, which was still a long way away.

Though I didn't know it at the time, that day I had reached the point in my climbing career where I didn't want to go further into the danger zone. My partner still wanted to push the envelope, so he continued, ticking off successful climbing objectives with new partners. I focused on my professional life, still climbing, but not at the edge of danger anymore.

Then one day I saw that I'd gotten a voicemail from him. I knew he was up in Alaska with a rather famous climber who was known to take risks that other people thought were way out there. His message said, basically, that he went to the edge of the void, stared at it, and decided it wasn't for him. He pushed past his limits to a place he didn't like. He hit that point, as I had, where the risk, suffering, pain, and fear were no longer worth it.

Our adventures continue though, and we still spend many a winter's day, dropping steep couloirs and tree skiing in the backcountry together, exploring new lines down unnamed mountain faces of the national forests. We are constantly going way too fast, crashing through branches, avoiding cliffs (mostly), and generally whooping it up together. Backcountry snowboarding allows me to still feel a little like a badass in order to keep the midlife crisis at bay. It also gives me some of my happiest moments.

I've pulled back from intense participation in most of the extreme sports that dominated my early adulthood. Now I get satisfaction and joy by immersing myself fully in whatever I'm doing, rather than from how dangerous it is, or how hard I have to push through fear and discomfort. There are times I look back at all the risks, all the close calls, and wonder how much of it was just boys being dumb. There is no question that I loved all the excitement and the challenges. They were the antidote for the dull pain of existence. But the question that I continue to ask myself as I get deeper into my fifties is, Did I manage to come through it all unscathed because of ability or just dumb luck? My answer varies depending on my mood, which means it's probably a healthy mix.

I had to go through all the adventures to learn how I wanted to live, and similarly, I needed to go through the relationship with Jane to be the person I am today. I realized early on that Jane couldn't really wrap her brain around the kind of emotional responses I was having to her lifestyle. But the relationship provided me with a mirror into myself.

My journey into non-monogamy had brought me to a point where I was comfortable with things I never thought possible. I have to say, given that when I started the journey, I had a hard time even *thinking* about Jane with another man, I was surprised by how relaxed I had gotten with it all. I had always desired a partner who would accept me for all my own weirdness, one from whom I wouldn't have to hide any part of my sexual desires or my need for adventure, and Jane was that person. Initially, I did try to fool myself by pushing the painful parts of her desire for other men out of my mind, but the reality is that I *like* feeling things, especially things that challenge me. Jane being Jane was far more of a challenge than I was prepared for. I need to be more careful about what I wish for. I just might get it.

***

When Jane and I officially split—which was kind of a public thing, as was everything else she did—many people said, "See, I told you that non-monogamy thing doesn't work." I roll my eyes at this, since about half of all marriages end in divorce, whether traditional or not. Do these same people think that the "monogamy thing" doesn't work either? To quote my favorite line from the movie *Bull Durham*, "The world is made for people who aren't cursed with self-awareness."

I would never recommend non-monogamy to anyone, but then again, I wouldn't recommend monogamy either. It's just a question of which problems would you rather have, as it seems to me, you're going to have them either way. Understanding that made the journey a lot more reasonable for me. I also recognized that non-monogamy gave me more of the kind of excitement in my life that I desired, and also forced the kind of growth I was most interested in. Monogamy might have forced me to learn how not to be a slave to my desires, but my desires are the rocket fuel my life thrives on. I'd much rather get burned a few times along the way than never get to see where a desire-fueled life might take me.

***

Jane and I didn't speak for almost a year after I left NYC, but when communication did start up again, the depth of our connection emerged from the ashes of our breakup. And once I started on this project, she was fully supportive and helped out in any way she could. She shared memories of events, provided feedback on the various drafts, and helped re-create our critical conversations. Our friendship continues to grow.

I have been struggling to come up with more details to flesh out the ending of the relationship, so you, the reader, are not left with the sense that it just sort of evaporated into thin air. But in reality, it's kind of appropriate since that's how it felt to me at the time. There was a sense of loss, but without its being tied to an event—no one died; she didn't meet someone new; she didn't come to me one day and say we're through; I didn't say, "I've had enough of this," and walk out. We just started slowly slipping away from each other until she was gone as my partner but still there as my roommate.

Even with all the struggles, my life with Jane is something I value. And as you've seen, if you've made it this far, it's had a dramatic impact on who I am. I know Jane feels the same way about our time together, proven by the effort she's made to stay close over the last two years. It's also worth noting that now solidly into her early forties, she is quite critical of some of her behavior back then. Not the sex, but the way she related to me at times. We've talked about it, and she now admits that she did treat me unfairly when it came to certain aspects of our relationship. She grew up with limited resources, emotional and psychological, and was forced to deal with adult social interactions and sexual scenarios as an early teen. She never really had a chance to learn how to give and receive love. In her own words: "I had to figure out on my own, how to take care of myself from a very early age. I learned that it was an 'every man for himself' world that I lived in, and if I didn't protect myself, nobody would."

Her remorse has helped heal some of my wounds from our journey together. She's onto the next phase of her life now, and although still very nonmonogamous, she's putting more energy into her careers in academia and media than into hookups and partying. I have been fully supportive of her new focus.

***

I ventured into the world of extreme non-monogamy because I found someone I wanted to be with who would only accept that relationship model. But the wild sex aside, I went on this journey because it scared me, and it was the kind of fear that told me there was something significant to be learned. It was a beautiful thing to finally see how much impact my demons had been having on my life. To look them in the eye and say, "I'm not going to let you have that hold on me any longer."

Not that I'm trying to say I'm fixed. The demons still take me down sometimes and it can be a struggle to get back up. But I always get back up.

I realized that I do not want the kind of open-as-fuck relationship that I had with Jane. It's just not what I need or want at this point. I found out that our relationship didn't return to me the things I did need, which was deep intimacy on my journey through life. Was that due to our relationship being open-as-fuck, or was it just that, regardless of the reasons, Jane had different intimacy needs than I did? I really don't know.

I've also realized I can't do basic monogamy either. The thought of having sex with only one woman for the rest of my life seems like a soul-killing sentence. I don't think I'd be capable of it. That said, I'd rather non-monogamy be more of an occasional treat than the prime directive, as it seemed to be for us. Something that helps keep the arousal level up and adds a little spice into life.

I believe this is currently called "open monogamy." I really like the sound of that.

***

I'm currently single and the battle of trying to convince myself I'm powerful and emotionally strong as I inch closer to my mid-fifties still goes on. Apparently, this will be a lifelong challenge for me. I have no idea what my next relationship will hold. I've seen in my post-Jane dating life how being honest about these experiences I've had has turned a few women off. But hiding who I am is no longer an option for me, and if I meet someone who doesn't approve of the choices I've made, well, then they're just not the right woman for me. Being able to have *that* attitude feels like I've taken one of the best parts of Jane and made it my own.

I do hope I've been eloquent enough for you to see that for me, the moral of this story is how much value there is in seeking the risk rather than the reward. And that my relationship with Jane was far more interesting, more profound, and yes, in the end, more rewarding than any safer, more traditional journey I might have taken.

This philosophy continues to motivate me to do the things I choose to do, be they business, athletic, or artistic endeavors. Hell, it even motivated me to write this, which was a challenge, given that it puts a lot of private details about me into the world. But my aversion to laying my experience bare was exactly why I knew I should do it. I also wondered whether telling my story might be of service to folks who are venturing into that world. Sometimes just knowing you're not the only one who struggles can help.

I don't think that I'm some great oracle, or that I've cracked the code on how to do open relationships. Being with Jane was a wild, fun ride, full of serious bumps, crashes, and, at times, outright personal devastation. It takes a sharp knife to get through tough skin, and extreme non-monogamy was about as sharp a knife as I could have found. It allowed me to look at my insides and see myself in all my humanness, failings, and beauty.

***

Going over the journal entries for the "Hitting My Stride" chapter was difficult for me. Those couple of years were a very happy time in my life. Thinking back upon those experiences made me miss Jane in a way I hadn't for a while, and it speaks to how good it was when we were in sync, and everything was firing on all cylinders. Again, I shudder to think that I would have missed out on all that if I had let my emotions get the better of me and had not taken the risk on the relationship with Jane.

I can't definitively say why I wrote this. It may be that I wrote the book I wish I had been able to read as I was getting deeper into my relationship with Jane. Or it may be that I wrote it to exorcise the demons that remained with me from that whole experience. Or perhaps it was out of pure narcissism and with the hope of gaining some notoriety. Bah, I could probably find evidence to support all of those reasons and several others.

But the writing experience itself turned out to be far riskier than I had imagined. What started out as a safe essay about the joys and pitfalls of non-monogamy, and strategies for navigating them, turned into an intensely challenging revisit of the journey I went on. Once again, I wasn't prepared for what I had gotten myself into, as the writing uncovered some deep emotions and pain that I was unaware still lingered.

As I got into it, it became clear that laying bare all that I felt, saw, and went through with Jane uncovered some truths that I had previously been unwilling to admit to myself. Ultimately, that process stimulated the rest of the healing.

Epilogue

I park the old truck at the cold and snowy trailhead and begin to put my ski boots on inside the cab while I leave the truck running to keep warm. Shortly, I turn the engine off and step into the quiet, still morning to take my skis out of the back. After fitting my boots into the bindings, each responding with a loud click when locked, I stride off into the woods, gliding effortlessly on the cold new snow. The snowboard is back at home. There is no destination today. No mountain to climb. No slope to judge the safety of. No danger zone to go into. No thrilling ride to cap off the morning's physical challenge. I'm just gliding through the woods for the sake of being outside, in the solitude of nature.

Jane and I were just two people who tried to make it work for a while, and most definitely did when we were at our best. I don't know how our friendship will develop over the next few years, but one thing is for sure, if it does continue, it won't be boring. We're not right for each other anymore, but our friendship has a closeness and depth that could only have come about through the journey we went on together. We both realize that.

Twenty years ago, you could not have paid me to be this calm on an outdoor excursion. But now, here I am, enjoying the peace and the relaxation. Mother Nature is presenting herself to me in all her beauty, just like she always did, I realize. The snow-frosted trees. The frozen creeks. The rabbits and birds that scurry away as I intrude into their world. My legs and arms kick off and glide over and over again, and I'm struck by the simplicity of the motion. Kick. Push. Glide. All four limbs in sync like a well-oiled machine propelling me through the snowy wilderness at an easy pace that is remarkably enjoyable.

I don't need to prove my strength or how much of a badass I am at every chance. I *am* strong; my needs *are* important; my feelings *are* real. Without Jane, I question how long I might have continued to go through life without realizing these things. Seeking the risk is how I have always lived my life, but I've finally learned that giving things the respect they deserve also applies to how I think of, and how I treat, myself.

I ski off into the snowy forest . . .

Acknowledgments

- Jane, for opening my eyes to a brave new world full of wonderful experiences.
- My climbing partner and best friend, without whom I would have achieved so much less in my life.
- The group of Idiots who shaped my early years (if you're wondering if I mean you, then I most certainly don't).
- Chicken and DFG, for always being by my side through the good, the bad, and the ugly times of Jane.
- My dad, for giving me his creativity and wanderlust.
- My mom, for giving me her curiosity.
- The Rock, for pushing me to take my notes and make a readable story out of it.
- All the close friends who have supported me in this endeavor. You know who you are.
- Special thanks to Brad Wetzler, who first convinced me I could write a better story, and then helped me go for it in ways I never thought I could.
- Double-secret extra-special thanks to my remarkable editor, who tirelessly acted as not only my editor, but confidant, therapist, coach, cheerleader, and friend. This work never would have existed without your unwavering commitment to the project.

Thank you all